IMAGES OF
ESSEX

Alfred Philip Wire, headmaster of Harrow Green School, May 1901.

IMAGES OF ESSEX

The Photographs of Alfred Wire 1875–1913

David Mander

VESTRY HOUSE MUSEUM

ALAN SUTTON PUBLISHING LIMITED

First published in the United Kingdom in 1995 by
Alan Sutton Publishing Ltd • Phoenix Mill • Far Thrupp • Stroud • Gloucestershire

Vestry House Museum • London Borough of Waltham Forest

British Library Cataloguing in Publication Data
A catalogue record for this book is available from the British Library.

ISBN 0-7509-1004-6

Cover photographs: (front) Stone Bridge, Chelmsford, 1893; Wharf, Bow Bridge, 1898; (back) Susan Wire and her daughter Agnes, 1904; (half-title): Skaters on the frozen pond at Wanstead Flats, February 1895; (title page): St John's Street, Colchester, June 1903; (this page): the castle at Colchester, taken in 1904 from the tower of St Nicholas Church, a vantage point not available to the modern photographer.

Typeset in 11/15 Baskerville.
Typesetting and origination by
Alan Sutton Publishing Limited.
Printed in Great Britain by
Butler & Tanner, Frome, Somerset.

CONTENTS

Agnes Wire and a friend, with a kitten, May 1896. This composition would have been a considerable challenge for the kind of stand camera Wire was using at this time.

ACKNOWLEDGEMENTS

In compiling this book, I have drawn on a wide range of printed sources on the history of Essex, the most useful of which were the Victoria County History volumes. Many people provided information and advice and I am grateful to the following: Roger Colori, Nigel Sadler, Gail Cameron and Jo Parker of LB Waltham Forest's Vestry House Museum; Richard Shackle and other staff at Colchester Library's local studies library; Howard Bloch and Dorcas Sanders of Newham Local Studies Library; Ian Dowling of Redbridge Local Studies Library; the staff of Essex Record Office and its branches at Colchester and Southend, especially Jane Bedford; Mr E.A. Harvey of Burnham-on-Crouch; the staff of Epping Forest District Museum; the dog walker in Willingale; and to all those local authors on Essex topics, living and dead, on whose knowledge and research I have drawn. Special thanks to Sue and Rod Fraser for hospitality. If any mistakes have crept in, I hope that my Essex readers will allow some indulgence to a trespasser from across the Lea.

Alfred Wire's photograph collection can be consulted by prior appointment at Vestry House Mueum, Vestry Road, London E17 9NH; tel 0181 509 1917. Copy prints can also be obtained from the museum; apply in writing to the Keeper for details.

Dedication

For Thomas, who may follow after

INTRODUCTION: THE ESSEX OF ALFRED WIRE

The ancient county of Essex, which is bounded by the Lea, Stour and Thames, has visible settlement remains going back to Roman times, when Colchester was the regional capital. The undulating landscape is poor in stone and this has strongly influenced local building styles, which have relied in the main on brick and timber. Under the Saxons, Essex was a kingdom, and it has two surviving Saxon churches at Bradwell and Greensted, both of which feature in this book. The Saxon King Harold refounded the abbey at Waltham Holy Cross and was taken there for burial after his defeat and death at the battle of Hastings. The medieval period saw extensive church construction which used imported stone for delicate tracery around windows and an ingenious mixture of local materials for the remainder of the building. Ancient towns like Colchester became boroughs, joined by other towns, including Harwich, while the importance of Chelmsford's market and position enabled it to rise to prominence and become the county town.

London has always had an influence on the development of Essex. From Tudor times the county was a popular place for the courtiers' country estates, and photographs of two large sixteenth-century houses built round courtyard plans, Belhus at Aveley and Hill Hall at Theydon Mount, are included here. The county is also rich in smaller houses, some dating back to the late medieval period. Many were to disappear in the late nineteenth and early twentieth centuries, and

were visited by Alfred Wire. Eighteenth-century prosperity led to refacings or rebuildings, especially in Essex towns, as the street scenes at Dedham and Harwich show. Some of the wealth that allowed this building came from coastal trade and industry, for although the cloth trade that had grown up in medieval times was in decline throughout the eighteenth century, new industries based on malting, brewing and corn milling provided local prosperity.

Before the mid-1830s, Essex had depended on its rivers and on roads – some of which were turnpiked, to meet transport needs. The first railway was authorized between London, Colchester and Norwich in 1836, and by 1889 almost all the modern network was completed, so only one line was recorded under construction by Wire. Railway links played a vital part in the development of coastal resorts at Clacton and Southend, although connection to the railway did not automatically lead to population growth for smaller towns and villages. More significant in this context were the agricultural depression, which began in the 1870s, and the growth of London. The collapse of agricultural prices led to many small farmers and farmworkers leaving the land, and many went to the expanding capital. The south-west part of the county saw rapid suburban growth – in 1801 only 14,000 of the county's 228,000 lived there, but by 1901 this had risen to over a half of the county's people. The former villages of Leyton, West Ham and Romford had all expanded, while suburban

'This way now!' Donkey boys waiting for custom at the Wanstead Flats Fair, 1900.

development had spread out as far as Woodford. It was not until 1965 that administrative changes brought much of south-west Essex into the Greater London area, but by the end of the nineteenth century some of the parishes bordering the River Lea were known as 'London over the border'.

This was Alfred Wire's Essex, a county whose railways, largely built in his lifetime, enabled him and his family to travel easily, but whose historic heritage was in the process of considerable change as old houses and their estates gave way to developers, and many town houses and public buildings were demolished. With his keen sense of history and his photographic skills, Wire gradually built up a fascinating record of a county in the course of change from the late 1880s to the years of Edwardian prosperity before the First World War.

BRINGING THE HOUSE DOWN: ALFRED WIRE AND HIS TIME

Schoolteacher, antiquarian, amateur geologist and scientist, lecturer, inventor and, at his death, the longest serving headmaster in England – Alfred Philip Wire was all of these and, in addition, was a keen photographer from the early 1860s. He spent most of his life in his native Essex, and it is his photographic record of that county that this book celebrates. He wears a serious look in all his surviving photographs, which is a pity, for what comes through from the reviews of his lectures is a portrait of a lively character, concerned to inform through entertainment. One of the many publications that Wire contributed to, *The Teachers Aid* of 26 July 1902, includes a marvellous piece on how to make a working model of a volcano. The mountain was made from sand, with the top shaped into an inverted cone, containing pea-sized fragments of metal sodium. These were then covered with sand and cold water was poured over it, producing 'smoke, tiny explosions and the whole affair is very pretty and effective'. Wire cautioned against the audience getting too close and advised the teacher to rehearse the experiment quietly (!) beforehand, but, 'managed carefully the experiment is free from danger and of course "brings the house down"'.

Alfred Wire was born on 15 October 1839, the third of six sons who were still at home in 1851. His father, William Wire, was a watchmaker who had a small shop at No. 3 Church Lane, Colchester. From a radical Nonconformist family, William Wire was active in radical politics in the town from 1835 to 1839, anticipating the Chartist movement in seeking changes to the franchise. A self-educated man, he emphasized the importance of adult education in the struggle, for, as he put it himself in a lecture to Colchester Chartists who had come together to form a Working Men's Association, 'There is a Mechanics Institute in the town open every night . . . and every member can go and read the newspaper and periodicals, and have the privilege of taking a book home to read to his family . . . Knowledge is power and you can command it; you would also be instructing your children and making yourselves better men for society, and doing everything to render you worthy of your franchise.'

The increasing militancy of Chartism alienated William Wire, and after 1839 he was inactive in politics, concentrating instead on antiquarian matters and the study of Colchester's Roman past. His knowledge was widely recognized, but deeply resented by the better-off antiquarians of the district, though they could not prevent him from building up a substantial collection of Roman objects, amassed almost weekly in the course of a burst of building development taking place at the time. William Wire sold items to finance further purchases, and when his efforts to establish a public museum failed in 1840, he set up his own. The troubles of his middle years, his own and his children's poor health, and the continuing financial burden incurred when he stepped in to guarantee a friend's business that then failed, forced him to sell off much of the museum. But he was able to resume his work again and kept a detailed diary of new finds and where they had come from, invaluable to future researchers.

A strong belief in the power of education and the need to impart it, a restless curious mind, an awareness of the social barrier imposed by a radical Nonconformist background: all of these factors must have influenced Alfred Wire, perhaps more than it did the other children. One son had become the only free scholar at the unreformed grammar school, and a battle between William and the schoolmaster in 1842 was instrumental in gaining wider access for local children and a wider curriculum. But in 1851 his eldest son was a cabinet-maker. Herbert, the next brother, was to travel out to Hong Kong in 1856, and it was left to Alfred Wire to take up the baton as a schoolmaster. This must have been a considerable struggle for his family to achieve, since William had found it increasingly hard to make ends meet and took on the job of postman to supplement his earnings. One day in April 1857 he had been unable to find a substitute to deliver his letters and had gone out himself, dying shortly after his return home. The *Essex Standard* raised a subscription to help his widow and her four remaining dependant children, and without this support it is possible that Alfred Wire would not have been able to take up his teacher training place at Battersea Training College in 1860.

Alfred qualified two years later with a first class certificate, together with another for Practical and Theoretical Chemistry. At some stage he had left his family Nonconformity for the Church of England, and he now began his long career in church schools. His first job was as headteacher of the small country school at Little Baddow (which appears on page 71). Wire was to continue as a headteacher through his entire teaching life, and notched up an English record of fifty-two years as a headmaster at his death in 1914.

These first years at Little Baddow coincided with the regulations introducing school log books. The young headmaster had considerable difficulty in filling his first volume. 'Progress indefinable' was his entry for 29 July 1863. Boys were punished for stealing robins' nests or had to stand on a desk for not knowing the name of Cain's brother. Wire congratulated himself for being able to prevent writing on walls, but in a rural community lessons had to be fitted round the seasonal demands of agriculture. Children could be kept away from school to pick peas, scare birds or help with the hay making. The

Susan Wire and her daughter Agnes, 26 May 1904.

Nelly Wire and feline friend, July 1905.

autumn of 1863 must have been especially uneventful, for at the end of October, Wire lapsed into verse, each couplet being the day's entry:

> While I am keeping this log book
> I might be teaching boys
> Or else employing every look
> To stop increasing noise.
> The children all are learning now
> I hope 'twill do them good
> For some of them will go to plough
> And some will fell the wood.

Alfred's efforts at class discipline seem to have paid off, as he was able to summarize the inspector's report for July 1863 as 'It is a nice village school of neat children, mostly young. The Master seems to work it well.' Relief was to come in October 1864, when Wire secured his first promotion and moved to Macclesfield. It may be that it was on the strength of this that he was able to marry Susan, a Norfolk woman two years his junior. Between 1866 and 1877 he taught in Macclesfield, Radwinter (Essex), Newmarket and Dunstable, before accepting the headship of a new board school in Leyton in 1877. He and his wife had five children between 1864 and 1877: Alfred, Ellen (1866), Arthur (1868), Agnes (1872) and Ernest (1875). Two more were born at Harrow Green: William (1880) and Ethel (1883).

Harrow Green was the third of Leyton School Board's new schools. The board had been established in 1874, when the parish only had two schools, but needed over 1,200 additional places for pupils. Wire recalled that when he first came to the district, the nearby Cannhall and Crownfield roads were country lanes, with fields on both sides, and butterflies flourished along Grove Green Road – when little boys were not out hunting them! The school opened on 14 May 1877 with one assistant master and 87 pupils. Expansion thereafter was rapid. At the beginning of 1879 there were 561 pupils in all three departments (boys, girls and infants), growing to

Ethel Horlock (née Wire) and child, 1909. This photograph may have been taken in the back garden of Wire's house in Birkbeck Road.

772 by the end of the school year, with the addition of a second storey to the main building. Further building raised capacity to 1,200 by 1882, an indication of the rapid growth in population as the surrounding area was built over and attendance rates from potential scholars improved.

We can glimpse life at Harrow Green School through the very thorough log books kept by Wire for the thirty-seven years of his headship. Life in the new district was much too busy for poems. Poor attendance was one of the problems he had to grapple with, leading in one case to a visit to Stratford Police Court in June 1877 when the parents of one child were prosecuted. Most parents made the struggle to meet the school fees, which were assessed in bands ranging from 2*d* to 1*s* for infants and 9*d* to 1*s* 6*d* for boys and girls, but in December 1879 Wire noted that many children had no school money to make the payments. Attendance was only the first stage of the process; once there the children had to be taught, and the new head had some lively ideas. The initial inspector's report of January 1878 noted that the school was in good order and the teaching creditable. Good behaviour was rewarded with treats – in November 1877 the boys were allowed out to watch Langers Circus pass along the High Road. And in September 1879 there is the first record of a special lecture: 'An hour with a candle'. The majority of Wire's special lectures were to be delivered with the aid of a lantern slide, and it would seem likely that his interest in photography grew from his practical need to keep the attention of his classes. Prize-giving days were also made into entertainments, taking place in December along with a Christmas programme of recitation and songs.

By 1882 the staff had grown to ten, including Wire's second son, Arthur. Wire had developed his lecture programme and was raising funds for a new library and a harmonium with topics like 'A lump of salt'. Truancy was still a problem, as was violence towards teachers. In February 1886 one pupil was caned for truancy and kicked, but Wire recorded that: 'I used the cane pretty freely to reduce him to submission.' Two other boys were caned and locked up in the school until collected by their fathers. In 1885 one child had 'a murderous weapon, using it to hit children'. Wire locked him in the upper lavatory but he jumped out of the window, and presumably escaped. Wire seems to have investigated problems and not

caned without cause. In June 1894 he recorded the reason for one child's absences: 'owing to both father and mother being locked up!! I suppose he will go to the Union', a reference to the grim workhouse building in Langthorne Road.

Relations between headmaster and the school board were usually good, but there were some hiccups. In October 1886 the chairman prohibited one of the forthcoming school entertainments. The vice-chair, Mr Birch, who was to prove a stout supporter of Wire over the years, had not been party to the decision and was able to overturn it. The resulting event, held in a nearby church Sunday School room, attracted more children than the room could hold. Wire was also granted time away to prepare lectures, and in October 1888 he visited the Tower of London as part of his research into Lady Jane Grey. A lecture to Standards 5 and 6 followed the next day.

The school attracted some good publicity – entry into national writing competitions, for example – and some less favourable. In October 1889 some pupils joined in a strike for 'no home lessons, no stick and no grammar', as a boy striker informed a passer-by. Wire found that the police were not prepared to help him, though they did eventually agree to send round a constable to the strikers' homes, but by the fourth day the whole affair was over.

Lectures were not Wire's only activity outside the confines of the classroom. He was an early member of the local photographic society, and supported the local Conservative party, though he declined several offers of standing for a seat on Leyton Local Board. He was a founder member of the Essex Field Club, serving as their honorary librarian for many years. He served on the committee of the Survey of London and many of his photographs were used in the early survey volumes. In turn, all of this activity fed lectures, given to a variety of audiences, ranging from learned societies to the children in the Mile End workhouse, where his illustrated rendering of traditional nursery stories 'kept his audience in a continual roar of laughter during the whole three hours'.

In the midst of this activity, Wire found time for a commercial venture. The Wire family's first Leytonstone home had been 13 Mornington Terrace on Union Road (later Langthorne Road), opposite the union workhouse. In March 1883 the

Wire's house in Birkbeck Road, Leytonstone. An undated snow scene probably taken in the 1890s. The tramway depot is on the left.

Harrow Green, Leytonstone, May 1897. This view is looking east from Leytonstone High Road. Harrow Road lies directly behind the shed that was to form a target for removal. Much development had taken place in the 1860s, and overcrowding combined with poor sanitary conditions resulted in a death rate greatly above the national average in the 1880s. A smallpox outbreak resulted in 98 cases and 24 deaths, mainly at Harrow Green. Frequent visits by Leyton's sanitary inspectors helped to bring about gradual improvements.

family moved just round the corner to 1 Seaton Villas in Birkbeck Road (later No. 168). The new house gave Wire more space, and he was able to establish his own laboratory. The property was to become registered to the Kreochyle Company.

Wire had entered into partnership with a Prof. Barff, and together they produced a liquid beef, derived from soluble albumen. The product was intended as a food for infants and in cases of sickness when solid foods would be rejected. The partners issued a prospectus in 1884 and Wire's son Arthur left his pupil teacher post at his father's school to help make and bottle the product. However, there seems to have been no second edition and the Kreochyle Company dissolved into history. Although a newspaper feature on Wire, written in 1898, implied that the liquid beef was still then in production, sixteen years later the obituary notice of its joint creator

made no mention of it. Perhaps the Kreochyle project helped Wire in his application to join the Chemical Industrial Society in the late 1880s.

The next decade was a busy one for Wire. In 1890 he launched a movement to establish a public library service in Leyton, and he saw the former Town Hall become the first public library in 1894. Wire was also concerned about the appearance of Harrow Green. As a local paper, the *Express and Independent*, put it in February 1898:

> Harrow Green does not justify its name, it is overcrowded with houses, themselves over-crowded; there is absolutely nothing green about it, except in the way of paint and were it not for the proximity of Wanstead Flats and the Forest, the inhabitants would be in much worse case than they are now.

A headmaster and his staff: Wire (third from left, front row) and colleagues in the yard at Harrow Green School, 29 May 1895.

A dancing bear and its keepers, Harrow Green School playground, 9 May 1890.

The solution lay in 'an unsightly triangular piece of ground which gives the locality its name, but which is as devoid of greenery as every other part of this ill favoured neighbourhood'. Wire was the secretary of Leyton's committee set up to celebrate Queen Victoria's Diamond Jubilee, and he proposed that the old wooden shed in the centre of Harrow Green be replaced with a fountain. Eventually Harrow Green got its fountain in 1901 and the shed was removed by Leyton Urban District Council. However, the committee were all left out of pocket as the appeal to the public to beautify Harrow Green had not met with the shower of funds they had expected.

Looking back towards the end of his life, Wire recorded that his first surviving photograph dated from 1861, but we have no print from this early period and much of his work dates from the 1890s. Wire's experiments in various techniques of taking and producing photographs led to the production of a number of short pieces for the *Amateur Photographer*. In 1894 George Philip and Son published *Knowledge through the Eye*, a joint work by Wire and George Day on the preparation and use of lantern slides in lectures. Over the next ten years, Wire produced articles on camera holders, developing tips and photographic book plates. He was becoming something of a local celebrity and was the subject of a *District Times* feature in May 1902, where the reporter called on him in his laboratory, 'surrounded by instruments for chemical experiments. Tiers of shelves on each side of the room were filled with neatly labelled boxes. These I learned later contained photographic negatives and lantern slides, all of them the result of his own work.' Wire recalled when Harrow Green had been a hiding place for London thieves, a stronghold of counterfeiters and was regarded as a plague spot by all decent citizens, but these times were far from over. Among the cuttings kept by Wire, there is a

Picture discovery: Wire's 'instantaneous picture', showing the playground of Harrow Green School, 1891.

curious account of a surprise visitor to the Wire household. One Friday evening in February 1890, Wire was woken at 11 p.m. by the barking of his dog. He let the dog out into the back yard and, following, found John Wistby, a Spitalfield costermonger, who had climbed over the gate and had 'nicely arranged some broken bottles and a board so that he could sleep' in Wire's shed. Wire called his neighbours and they established that the man was neither drunk nor dangerous, but had recently been released from prison. Eventually the police arrived and took the confused Wistby away.

Wire became the first president of Leyton Teachers Association in 1895, formed as a breakaway association from the South Essex Association of National Teachers, which the Leyton teachers had objected to on the grounds that it had adopted 'low class trade unionism tactics'. He continued to write pieces for the educational press and locally gave the benefit of

his wisdom to the new association. In June 1902 he delivered a paper on 'The Co-ordination of Primary and Secondary Education', a wide-ranging discourse taking as its starting point the forthcoming Education Act (then still in the bill stage), and exploring the key issues of the balance between keeping pupils interested and ensuring that the basics were taught thoroughly.

The Education Act led to the abolition of school boards. In Leyton the management of local education was taken over by the Education Committee of Leyton Urban District Council, with many of the old board members joining the new committee. This was to show up in October 1904, when Wire was sixty-five and ordinarily would have retired. It is certain that he wished to carry on and, after discussion, the Education Committee resolved to extend his service for a further year. Councillors objected, but under pressure from Wire's supporters their opposition was dropped and Wire stayed on. He had been headmaster for thirty-seven years; many of his staff had passed through the school as pupils and it was difficult to imagine Harrow Green School without him. Wire also had a powerful sense of duty, and in the event he was to serve the school and district he loved for a further nine years.

Wire had seen his children established in their careers and families. One son had become a member of Leyton's Education Committee and was later to take up the post of Principal of Christ's College, Blackheath, and in May 1913 Wire was away from school to attend the inaugural meeting of a photographic society at the college. Wire's wife, Susan, died in 1911, but it is likely that one or more daughters continued to live at home and look after him. In 1913 signs of illness and fatigue began to appear. In November he was unwell with prostrate trouble, but he was fit enough in December to attend a meeting of the Committee for the Survey of Monuments of Greater London. In February 1914 his illness returned and he was away

between 3 and 9 February, noting on his return that he 'was not up to much work, but the state of the first class needed my presence as Head to do work the supply teachers ought to have done'. He attended a meeting of the London Society in March, but was taken ill on 7 April and did not return until 29 April, when he came in for a short while and 'the boys were very pleased to see him'. But on 4 May he was forced to take sick leave, and ten days later he missed the thirty-seventh anniversary of the founding of the school – the first time he had ever been away from this celebration. Four days later he was granted three months' sick leave, and he died peacefully at home on 12 June 1914.

A special assembly was called at the school, and one of the teachers told the boys 'how proud we felt at having been associated with such a gentleman who had the welfare of his boys so much at heart, the splendid example he had set by his exemplary life and the good he had done for the district in which he had resided for so many years'. The funeral, six days later, at

Harrow Green School, March 1896. Regular sport and exercise was an important part of the curriculum. Here the boys of Standard 5 are at their drill.

The girls' playground at Harrow Green School, May 1897. Victorian schoolchildren were only usually caught on camera in formal groups or seated properly at their desks. Wire has captured the noise and games that went on outside the lessons, and just a hint of whispered confidences at the water pipe.

Harrow Green Church, was attended by the entire staff and 180 boys, who filled half of the church. Besides the family, the gathering included eight Leyton councillors, the Leyton town clerk, representatives from the many bodies that Wire had served on and teachers from ten local schools. After the service the boys marched behind the funeral carriages to West Ham Cemetery and the school choir sang hymns, including Wire's favourite: 'Oh God, our help in ages past'. At his death he was England's longest serving headmaster, having enjoyed a career of fifty-one years.

Wire left a substantial collection of photographs, lantern slides, books and cuttings volumes to his children. This treasure trove appears to have been divided between two of the sons, Arthur and William. Arthur's part, the bulk of the collection, was in the South of France by

1934 and seems to have been lost. William inherited the Leyton and Essex material, and this was to form two donations to Leyton Library. The first, in 1934, consisted of 675 photographs and nearly 200 lantern slides, and covered much of the county of Essex, not just Leyton. The second, in 1940, added a further 700 lantern slides, the bulk of those used by Wire in his lectures on Essex local history. The evidence of articles that appeared in the *Amateur Photographer* and in local papers suggested that Wire had taken many other photographs on holidays in other areas of England, and this material would appear to have been retained by Arthur Wire, or given away to some of the societies or other bodies he had links with. William seemed to believe that anything that remained had gone with Arthur to France and must be presumed lost. Even in this diminished form, Leyton was able to record that it had received over 1,233 negatives, making the Wire bequest its largest holding of photographic material from a single donor.

William did not mention that his donation to Leyton also included the bulk of his father's library collection on Essex historical subjects. This included two substantial series of cuttings books on Wire's own activities and on Essex matters that caught his attention, and these were indexed by Leyton Library. There were over four hundred volumes in all.

Harrow Green School did not long outlast its innovative and long-serving headmaster. In 1929 it was condemned, and three years later it was remodelled to become an infant school, closing altogether in 1935. The four very substantial log books, swelled by copies of the programmes of

Wire's entertainments and lectures, found their way into the offices of Leyton Town Hall and thence to the public library's local history collection. Leyton's archives and local history library was put into store during the Second World War, while the reference library served as a citizens advice bureau, but after 1945 the collections were brought up from the basements and catalogued. Prints were produced from the negatives (which had accompanied the photographs), and, mounted on green card, these formed a part of the expanding photograph collection built up on Leyton and Essex parishes.

It was at Leyton Library in the late 1970s that I first came across the work of Alfred Wire. From the early 1980s the Leyton local history collections were gradually moved to Vestry House Museum, which had become the record office for

The race is about to start for Harrow Green schoolchildren at the Jubilee Sports, June 1897. Without proper sports grounds, races had to be held in the street, but with so little traffic this does not seem to have been a problem. Harrow Green School pupils competed against other schools, and the log book records pupils attending a regional children's sports day at the Spotted Dog public house at Upton in 1891. The Jubilee Sports of 1897 were a purely local event.

Harrow Green schoolboys on a nature walk, summer 1904. Wire's many pioneering initiatives included nature study. Standard 5 and their master, Mr Hall, are about to set out through the forest.

the London Borough of Waltham Forest, and which also holds a large visual collection on the area. In the years that followed, some of Wire's photographs appeared in print or in exhibitions, but the significance of his work across the old county of Essex was largely forgotten. With the changes in local government in 1965, when the old Essex areas of 'London over the border' became the London boroughs of Barking and Dagenham, Havering, Newham, Redbridge and Waltham Forest, the impetus for the new authorities to continue collecting for the old county gradually declined. Waltham Forest inherited two county-wide collections, but lack of resources and space to store them and allow public access prevented development. As a result the majority of those interested in the history of Essex have no knowledge of Wire and his work and will, I hope, find much to surprise and delight them in this selection from his images of the Essex of a hundred years ago.

THE PHOTOGRAPHIC TECHNIQUES OF ALFRED WIRE

Although a number of Wire's technical articles on photography have survived, we do not have a complete record of when he first started to take prints, or the methods he used. The earliest photograph in this collection dates from before 1875, but Wire was also making a great number of copy prints using a stand from the late 1890s onwards for his lecture purposes, so it is more likely that his earliest works date from the 1880s. This is the era when photographic techniques had developed sufficiently to make photography possible for the dedicated amateur, and Wire was more skilled than most, with his keen interest in chemistry and in experimenting.

Photography dates back to the 1830s, and by the 1850s prints were either made from glass plate negatives by the wet collodion process or from paper negatives. Until the later years of the

Harrow Green schoolgirls in a tableau, 20 June 1911. No school year would have been complete without its celebration of Empire Day each May. Britannia, flanked by Scotland and Ireland, rises above a selection of peoples from those parts of the map firmly coloured red.

nineteenth century, most prints were the same size as the negatives, then the introduction of enlargers allowed the easy production of larger prints. The earliest lantern slide dates from 1849, but it became increasingly common from the late 1880s as a lecturing aid. Wire was to be a pioneer in the production of lantern slides by the able amateur photographer.

Wire would have used a variety of stand cameras, using half- and quarter-plate negatives. The photograph of Wire with colleague George Day out in the snow (page 18) gives some idea of the sort of equipment he used, and the amount of gear he would have needed to carry round with him. At the beginning of 1898, Wire bought one of the new model hand cameras that were then

coming onto the market. After looking through advertisements in the technical press and talking to friends, he chose a Kodak Bulls Eye, which gave $3\frac{1}{2}$ inch square pictures from cartridge negatives. Wire found the new size perfect for lantern slides, but he also made his own prints directly from the negatives. In August 1898 he wrote up his first six months of filming for the *Amateur Photographer*. There had been some failures, but Wire felt that they were largely his fault, not those of the camera he was using. Compared with his old stand camera, he had achieved some good results for street views and snapshots, and he was especially pleased with his seaside views. The limitations of the Bulls Eye came with dull lighting and shade, so for very narrow streets or forest glades the longer exposures of the stand camera were better. Few photographs taken outside with the Bulls Eye survive.

Wire did not document the processes he used for printing up in his early years. He may have started with gelatine dry prints. These were the first negatives that could be used dry, being made up of light-sensitive silver halides suspended in a gelatine emulsion, which never completely dried out. They were stored in the dark until used. Ready made plates were available from 1878, and during the 1880s completely ousted the earlier wet collodion processes. But by the 1890s, in common with many amateur photographers, Wire had moved on to printing out paper (POP) and bromides. The POP process used a paper coated with silver chloride in gelatine, which was then contact printed and given a toner before being fixed and washed. Chronologically they were gradually replaced by silver bromide prints, composed of a silver halide developed-out paper,

in which silver bromide was suspended in a gelatine emulsion. These papers were faster than the POP process and also easily enlarged.

Once his prints were completed, Wire used a press to flatten them, then a white wheaten starch paste to mount them onto card or in albums. Wire did rather more than the average amateur photographer of the day when it came to lantern slides. Initially he had stuck to a half-plate stand camera, which gave good results and allowed the production of lantern slides by reduction. But these had to be made by artificial light. Wire had limited space at his disposal, and wanted to find a method that would allow a shorter exposure time, evening work and the production of a dozen or more slides quickly without a high percentage of failures. He was not convinced that the way for him lay with the slower, wet plate processes that many of his contemporaries in the mid-1890s were still using, but he also found that the commercially produced dry plates were too slow

A demonstration of flag waving by Harrow Green infants, 20 June 1911.

The benefits of the Bulls Eye camera: Messrs Hall, Hughes and Poole, teachers at Harrow Green School, and some of their charges, Mayville Road, 1901.

for his needs. So he made his own plates using a backing composed of caramel and burnt sienna, to which a thin piece of glazed brown paper was applied. His light source came from a gas burner and he used white paper, treated with a Chinese white as a reflector. Two shades and a home-made negative holder completed the equipment, and the exposure could then be made. The brown paper washed off in the developing fluid (again Wire made up his own, consisting of distilled water, potassium bromide, washing soda crystals, potassium carbonate and sodium sulphite). The lantern slide was finished off with a diamond cutter – this resulted in perfect centring of the

image within the resulting square of glass each time – and black needle-paper was then used for masking.

Some of Wire's original prints survive in the former Leyton collection, both in black albums, possibly put together by Leyton Library staff in the 1930s, but perhaps including some examples of Wire's own work, and mounted up onto the inimitable green card. However, many examples are now only represented by modern prints from the quarter-plate negatives, which constitute the bulk of what survives. Wire's substantial collection of lantern slides is all his own work. Some are original works – or at least no print survived to be

George Day and Wire caught by a fellow enthusiast setting up their stand camera for a winter study, 1895.

given to Leyton Library in 1934. Others are copies of his own photographs, of engravings or of earlier photographic works.

Wire also perfected his own stand for photographing objects, again mostly for use in lectures. Twenty-two photographs of finds at Colchester Museum – of particular interest to Wire, since many of them would have been through his father's hands in the 1840s and 1850s – may well have been taken using this special stand, but it would have played a great part in his lectures for children and his own pupils at Harrow Green School.

SUBJECT-MATTER

The bulky equipment needed for outdoor photography, combined with Wire's work, played a considerable role in the places he visited and what he chose to photograph. A schoolmaster had long holidays available, but he also had his family to think of. Wire could and did make special trips to places that interested him, and which would have required the services of a local horse and cart to reach. A documented example is the photograph of John Brown's house in Stanway, on the London road out of Colchester towards Coggeshall. Wire had visited the retired stonemason as a youth and returned when writing a memoir of his old friend in 1890. Many of his trips would have been with the Essex Field Club, and his antiquarian interests resulted in the camera being turned on the oldest buildings. This has produced some fascinating results for posterity, showing St Peter's on the Wall at Bradwell before later restoration, and offers a record of some of the larger houses of southern Essex before they vanished for good. But it also resulted in many views of Essex churches, the majority of which had already undergone substantial mid-Victorian restorations and reconstructions, so that they do not appear markedly different today.

Although Alfred intended to change from a stand to a hand camera, almost all his surviving work used the older equipment. His earlier street views are static, sometimes with a carefully posed horse and cart, but often no people. Where he did take 'instant action' shots, as in the boys playing leapfrog in Harrow Green playground (page 10), there is inevitable blurring, though a great impression of movement. The stand camera could produce good results – the view of the bear and its keepers in the school playground (page 9), also taken in 1890, is a case in point. Never one to waste an occasion, Wire then went on to give the children a lesson on the bear's anatomy, making the most of his small fee paid to the bear keepers to keep themselves and the animal still. But his later work is more lively, as we can see from the Post Office section of the Lifeboat Saturday parade in Colchester in 1903 to the seaside shots at Southend in 1910.

Wire continued to take a camera with him on family visits and holidays, and as a result the Wire daughters can be seen in a number of the compositions. Perhaps the most successful example is the view of the old gateway at Waltham Abbey, with his wife and two daughters posed by the fence, having just walked on while he took the photograph. In the same series they can be seen walking just ahead in the street views. But we can also be grateful for his interior work, notably the splendid view of the hall at Hill House, Theydon Mount, where the owner's pictures are either just about to go up, or to come down, as a move is clearly in progress.

Inevitably my selection of Wire's work would not have coincided with his own. I have been economical with the ecclesiastical and have spared the Roman pot, fascinating as these photographs are as a museum record. I have also included almost all of the industrial scenes, though these may have been taken for reasons of an adjacent antiquity rather than as a record of working life. There are many examples of Wire's sense of a good picture, either static compositions, like the distant scene of the quay at Mistley, or the wonderfully evocative instant pictures at the fairs at Mistley and Wanstead Flats. What are harder to explain are the gaps in the collection. There are no views of Maldon – though Chelmsford, Burnham on Crouch and Clacton are all featured – nor does Wire appear to have visited Saffron Walden or any of the little villages of north-west Essex, except for Castle Hedingham (not included in this book). It is possible that he did make a visit with a camera, but the photographs went with the other parts of the collection to the South of France – at present there is no way of knowing.

Naturally those parts of Essex closest to Leyton were easiest to reach, and as a result there is a substantial record of 'London over the border' and the adjacent areas. I have been selective in parts, notably with the many views of the Broadway, Stratford, decked out for a variety of celebrations in the early years of this century, but a lot of what Wire chose to photograph has changed or vanished. And progress has not been confined to the urbanized areas of the county; in many cases I have visited the towns and villages featured in this book to compare the modern scene, and the most difficult view to place was a village street in north Essex.

The selection that appears in this book has had to be made without Wire's own commentary. There are views where we can see why he was there and what he was doing, but there are many where this is not the case. I have tried to provide some background information and in some cases have taken the story forwards to link with the present. A note on sources and thanks to those who have helped with this book appear at the back. Any mistakes remain firmly my own. Many readers will start with a background and affection for Essex. I have come to discover the county as a result of opening a dusty green filing cabinet one day some seventeen years ago and being surprised and delighted with the vivid photographs that emerged. This book seeks to give Alfred Philip Wire and his Essex of a hundred years ago a new audience among the present-day people of Essex and all those who are interested in the history of the county.

Colchester High Street looking east from the Corn Exchange in 1874, with St Runwald's Church visible in the distance. The cab has just passed the old Town Hall.

St Runwald's Church, at the east end of the High Street, not long before it was demolished in March 1878. The church dated from the late thirteenth century and was one of a number of buildings cleared for traffic improvements by the Town Council.

COLCHESTER AND DISTRICT

The old St Nicholas Church from the Culver Street side. This is one of the earliest views in the collection. Dating from the fourteenth century, the church was undergoing restoration in 1708 when part of the tower fell onto the chancel. Work did not resume again until 1721, when the western end of the church was repaired. The timber-boarded tower was added in 1728, but the rest was left ruined. This view must date from before 1875, for then the old church was wholly cleared away, to be replaced by a new one designed by Sir Gilbert Scott and completed in 1876. This was to remain a place of worship until 1952 and was demolished three years later. St Nicholas House, incorporating a parade of shops, stands on this site today, but the graveyard on the Culver Street side of the churchyard remains.

The west end of the High Street, Colchester, August 1903. Cabs wait for hire outside the Essex and Suffolk Insurance Society offices. Built in 1820 and known as the Fire Office, this building adjoined Colchester's Corn Exchange. This photograph was taken a year before the electric tram tracks were laid along the High Street. On the left are two soldiers – a reminder of the importance of the barracks for the town's economy during the years of the late Victorian agricultural depression.

The High Street, Colchester, 27 June 1903. This was the intended site of the Grand Theatre, including the former Lamb inn. Work had begun in 1901 but was delayed when the first proposals were rejected by the Borough Council. The theatre, with seats for 700, was finally opened in 1905. It lasted a mere fifteen years before becoming a cinema, going on to change to a bingo club in 1961 and then reopening as a nightclub in 1990.

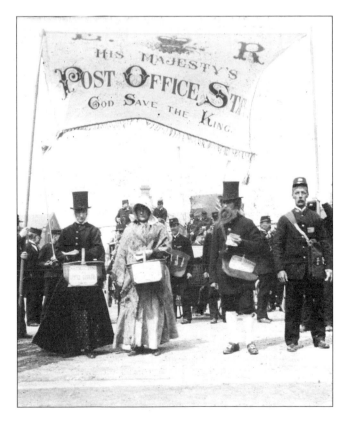

The flags are out for Lifeboat Saturday procession in the High Street, Colchester, 27 June 1903. A procession started from the Royal Artillery Barracks Square. The bottom view shows the contribution of the Colchester Postmen's Federation, and included one man dressed as the Colchester letter carrier of the 1850s, the job that Wire's father had held. In the evening there was an illuminated fête and fireworks in the castle grounds. The *Essex Standard* felt that never before had Colchester seen such an elaborate and extensive pageant, with good behaviour from the crowds, no drunkenness and perfect weather.

The Red Lion Hotel, Colchester, August 1904. Dating from between 1470 and 1500, the Red Lion now has its timbered beams exposed. Inside, the grill room still possesses moulded beams and carved brackets. During alterations to the building in the last year of William Wire's life, a Roman pavement was found below the yard. It was important enough to gain a place on the Ordnance Survey map, but the owner was not persuaded to halt the work or allow it to be lifted.

Colchester High Street, looking east from just beyond the Red Lion Hotel, August 1903. W. Hunt & Sons had just taken over from Pecks and had a further thirty-one years trading ahead of them. The second St Nicholas Church spire rises in the middle distance, with All Saints Church in the background.

Colchester High Street, looking west towards the new Town Hall, June 1903, with a few market stalls in evidence on the left.

This is Colchester's second town hall, built on the site of its medieval predecessor in 1845 but felt to be inadequate as early as 1878. It included a large assembly hall, a courtroom and chambers for the magistrates, together with a police station and cells. Two courtrooms were added in 1882 and neighbouring property was acquired for further extensions, but in the event a new town hall was commissioned.

The old Town Hall was demolished in 1897 and construction of its successor, designed by Sir John Belcher, was well under way by 1899, when this photograph was taken. The 162 foot high tower has come to be a feature of the town. The finished building was opened by the Earl of Roseberry in 1902.

St Mary's Steps and Church, Colchester, 1899. This view is from what was then Balkerne Lane. St Mary's late Perpendicular tower rises above the cottages, and to the left is a corner of the church school. This had begun as a Sunday and Dame School in 1859, and moved to the building on Balkerne Lane in 1864, after the Rector of St Mary's, C.A.L. Oste, had donated the site and a public subscription had paid for the building. An infant school opened here in 1873. Despite overcrowding, it continued to be supported by subscriptions and government grants until competition from School Board and later local authority schools brought about its closure in 1930. This scene changed radically with the construction of the ring road, and the cottages and school had gone by 1980.

Young boys pausing for the camera in Eld Lane, near the Schere Gate, Colchester, June 1903. Now part of a pedestrian area, this part of Eld Lane and Sir Isaac's Walk retains most of the timber-framed houses and small town properties seen in this view. A pedestrian gate existed at this point in the city walls in the thirteenth century, and houses were built up against it by 1436. Houses were built over the gate during the late fifteenth century and the last of the wall had been robbed for domestic building by 1694, when only the houses and the narrow passage preserved the position of the medieval gateway.

It looks as if the same boys have gone down through the Schere Gate and are now playing outside Studd's Grocery. Fresh air is being let into Gorham the bootmakers at 45 St John's Street.

St John's Street, Colchester, looking east, August 1904. Wire was a frequent visitor to Colchester and took this photograph just along from Studd's shop, with the Brewers Arms public house in the middle distance. St John's Street was known as Southsherde Street in the late fourteenth century and more directly in the mid-eighteenth century as Gutter Street, from the large gutter that ran down the centre of the road.

Tymperleys, Colchester, 13 June 1908. This house dates from the fifteenth century. Wire took this photograph looking back towards the gateway through to Trinity Street. This building once formed part of a larger house, having a hall range that ran parallel with the street. It is associated with Dr William Gilberd (1544–1603), physician to Queen Elizabeth I, the first man to study electricity and give it a name. Extensive renovations have taken place since 1908, including the removal of the plaster covering to expose the beams. Tymperleys became a clock museum in 1987, run by Colchester Council, and houses the collection of the late Bernard Mason.

Opposite Tymperleys, on the other side of Trinity Street, is Holy Trinity Church, seen here in June 1903. The tower is the only surviving Anglo-Saxon structure in Colchester, though it incorporates a great many recycled Roman bricks. The body of the church dates from 1886, but some features of the earlier building have been retained. The church is now the Social History Museum.

The Old Grammar School, at the east end of Culver Street, Colchester, August 1903. The trees mark the back of All Saints churchyard. This grammar school was first mentioned in 1206 and was refounded by Henry VIII. The limitations of the curriculum in the 1830s led William Wire, the father of the only free scholar, to complain to the Bishop of London. Some changes were made including a move to new premises in London Road in the 1850s. The old school was taken over by Adams the coachbuilders and were later used as a garage, before being cleared in the 1970s. The site now forms the rear entrance to a supermarket.

St John's Abbey gate from St John's Green, Colchester, August 1903. The fifteenth-century north gatehouse of the Benedictine abbey founded in 1096 was extensively restored in the nineteenth century. The adjoining building is Gimber Cottage, dating from 1823.

St Botolph's Street, Colchester, looking north from St Botolph's Church Walk, August 1903. Bomb damage in February 1944, together with later redevelopment, has altered the street line. The printers and all of the shops visible as the street curves round have gone, but the pair of red-brick three-storey shops, two of the smaller shops beyond and the imposing four-storey block survive.

The east end of the High Street and the top of East Hill, Colchester, August 1903. The gabled building is the Gate House, dating from about 1600 and with a plaster front of around 1680. It is reputed to have been one of the establishments making bay and say. This was a serge-like cloth, originally woven by Dutch and Flemish refugees, though the trade had virtually died out by the early 1800s. The Gate House is now a health centre and offices for Colchester Borough Council.

This 1903 view from the top of East Hill includes East Hill House which dates from the early eighteenth century and whose top storey was added in about 1742. Beyond is St James the Great, whose tower was built in the thirteenth century. The cupola was added during a seventeenth-century restoration.

The Old Siege House, East Hill, Colchester, August 1907. At first sight only the tram tracks mark this view of the bottom of East Hill as a period scene. Colchester's trams had the briefest of lives – from 1904 to 1929, when they were replaced by buses. In 1900 this fifteenth-century building (far left) was still plastered over and divided into two shops. Since this photograph, however, the building adjoining it has also had its plaster removed to extend the black-and-white range. The Old Siege House is now a public house and restaurant.

Another seemingly unchanged sight is St Martin's Church, West Stockwell Street, Colchester, August 1903. This church suffered rather more damage during the 1648 siege of Colchester than the Old Siege House. The tower, built with considerable use of Roman bricks, was not restored after the bombardment. The body of the church, dating from the fourteenth century, was last used for worship in 1952. After 1958 it served as St Martin's Centre for plays and community activity, and it is currently unused.

West Stockwell Street, Colchester, August 1903. This is the 'Dutch Quarter', to the north of the High Street. This photograph was taken level with the house where James and Ann Taylor lived from 1796 to 1811; they were the authors of *Poems for Infant Minds*. The adjoining houses, Nos 13–16, date from the seventeenth century. The group of gables at the bottom of the street on the right are now the Stockwell Arms public house. The next houses, further up the hill with the raised steps, have been replaced with a modern building.

Maidenbury Street, Colchester, April 1899. This photograph was taken further east, from the junction between Maidenbury Street and St Helans Lane. The building on the right with attic windows was once a cloth warehouse, which became Colchester's first national school in 1812. Growing pupil numbers led to a move to a new building on St Helans Lane in 1861. Just beyond the former school is the Fencers inn, which was in its last year of operation as a public house. Today all the buildings survive, with alterations to doors and windows, as private houses.

The top of North Hill, Colchester, 1903. The gabled building beyond the Union Jack with the large bay on the first floor is the Wagon and Horses public house, which was later rebuilt. Lloyd's shop, next door, has had its eighteenth-century frontage removed, and the timbered beams of the older house further down the hill have been exposed.

North Bridge, Colchester, August 1903. The resolution to widen North Bridge was debated and passed by Colchester Borough Council in February 1903 as part of a scheme to widen the main road between the bridge and the railway station. Six months after the council meeting, Wire was on hand to record council workmen in action. Beyond the bridge, one of the cottages is being demolished as part of these works.

St Leonard's Church, Colchester, 1903. The fourteenth-century tower of St Leonard's, Hythe, is just visible above the churchyard trees. The Hythe was the old port of Colchester and the terminus of the 1904 tram route. Trading activities even spilled into the churchyard in 1594, when a man was prosecuted for making sails there. The battlements were added to the tower in 1748, and a later restoration followed in 1860. The timber-framed house alongside, now 133 Hythe Hill, has been altered in recent years.

An inspection is about to begin at one of Colchester's barrack parade grounds, August 1899.

St Mary the Virgin, Wivenhoe, August 1903. The fifteenth-century tower of this parish church is topped by an eighteenth-century cupola, but the body of the church was rebuilt in 1860.

John Brown's House, later Judd's Farm, Stanway, March 1890. Wire had been a frequent visitor as a young man, when the owner was the retired stonemason John Brown (1780–1859). Brown bought the farm in 1830 and built up a substantial natural history collection, teaching the young Alfred how to use a microscope. Brown's experiments with a burner once cost him the whiskers on one side of his face in a small explosion, but he was undeterred. Wire was writing a memoir of his old mentor in 1890 and would have been pleased that the farm survives today, behind a thick hedge.

The Church of St Mary the Virgin, Dedham, *c*. 1897. This church, situated on the Black Brook that runs down to the River Stour, is close to an old ford, which was the lowest that could be crossed at any season. Dedham was on the main road between Colchester and Ipswich and was one of the weaving centres that grew rapidly in the fifteenth century, benefiting from Flemish immigrants. South of the village is a rare survival – a medieval cloth factory, parts of which date from the twelfth century, with extensions of the early fifteenth century. It was wool money that helped to fund the splendid church, which replaced an earlier building in 1492. This view from the east end shows the tower, which was built from local knapped flint in 1519. The area was strongly Protestant in the reign of Queen Elizabeth I, and a lectureship was established in the 1570s to provide additional preaching. The second appointee was known as Roaring Rogers, who attracted crowds of up to 1,200 during the reign of King James I.

ALONG THE STOUR

Dedham, October 1897. On the opposite side of the road that skirts round the churchyard is the sixteenth-century Sun inn, whose coaching yard still has its unusual external timbered staircase. The arch of the yard came under threat in 1938 and the Dedham Vale Society was formed to fight a successful battle to save it from demolition. To the east the village shop is now a chemists, and beyond, a part of Sherman's Hall is just visible below the tree.

The street façade of Sherman's Hall, Dedham, hides a delightfully jumbled roofline. Since this photograph was taken in October 1897 the empty niche has had an urn replaced in it, recording the construction date of 1675 and the names of the owner and his architect – Thomas Sherman and Marshall Sisson. Three Sherman cousins emigrated to America in 1630, and a later descendant featured in the Declaration of Independence. The same family produced the American Civil War general, William Sherman.

The High Street, Dedham, looking east, August 1907. This photograph was taken from the junction with Mill Lane looking towards the Victorian Congregational Church, now an arts centre. To the left is the Marlborough Head inn, which was built in about 1500, then plastered over. Its timbers are now exposed again. To the right and just visible behind the trees is Dedham Grammar School, where headmaster Thomas Grimwood's extension of 1732 is marked by an inscription above the door. John Constable was one of Grimwood's pupils. The roadsweeper has done his work as the village street testifies – he has left his hand dustcart and departed for some well earned refreshment.

The north side of the High Street, Dedham, on the same day. The grocers is now the private Loom House, while the house at the end of the row is Brook House, which dates from the late fifteenth or early sixteenth century.

Dedham Mill, looking west along the mill stream, August 1907. This was the second mill on the site since Constable's time and was destroyed in a fire not long after Wire's visit. The present building of 1908 was the last working flour mill on the River Stour and has now been converted into flats, with a new block added alongside in 1987.

St Mary's Church tower, Dedham, forms the centrepiece for this photograph from the Suffolk side of the River Stour, 1905.

Just under two miles down river from Dedham is Flatford Mill and Bridge, in Suffolk. In this summer view, probably on the 1907 trip, it looks as though Wire's family have obligingly posed for him. The National Trust, who own the mill and bridge, have provided rather more regular handrails, and built a thatched shop just to the east of Bridge Cottage.

Manningtree is the smallest parish in Essex. Five of its twenty-two acres are under water at high tide. This is part of its very short High Street, looking from its junction with Brook Street, in August 1904. Today the White Hart public house has lost its resting stag and gained an off licence. It was once the halting place for stagecoaches. The town had its right to hold a market granted in 1238. A later infamous inhabitant was the seventeenth-century Matthew Hopkins, the self-proclaimed Witchfinder General, who died here in 1647.

The High Street, Manningtree, looking west, August 1904. Hammond's shoe shop, in the distance, is still trading today. The nearest public house with the projecting light is the Crown. Closer to Hammonds, the projecting blinds mark the site of the Packet Hotel, whose guests could go straight out of the back door onto a steamer bound for Harwich. A bookshop now occupies the site. On the other side of the road a buttress is all that remains of St Michael and All Angels' Church, parts of which dated back to 1616, and which was demolished in 1966.

The Swan Basin and the Grape Vine inn, Mistley, April 1899. Mistley owes its current appearance to the second Richard Rigby, who intended to make Mistley a spa and commissioned the architect Robert Adam to build the Swan Basin in 1776. The Grape Vine inn was originally the office for the maltings on the quay, though by the date of Wire's visit it was a public house. The building alongside was once the maltsters' sack-mending shed. Now the inn has become four cottages and the shed is a craft workshop.

The ruins of St Mary's Church, Mistley, April 1899. The twin towers were designed in 1776 by Robert Adam as an addition to the second St Mary's of 1735. When the nave of this church was demolished in 1870, to be replaced with a new church further inland, the towers were saved, either as mausoleums, or as landmarks for shipping in the estuary. Today they are in the care of English Heritage.

Two views of the High Street, Mistley, August 1904 (above) and 1903, showing the Thorn Hotel and Mistley High Street, with Mistley Towers in the distance. The building containing the Thorn Hotel and the post office has now lost its splendid first-floor bay, but otherwise the street remains intact. Behind the camera is a malting building, where the barley grains were soaked in water prior to germination and were then kiln dried. Surely then, as now, a rich chocolatey smell of malt would have penetrated the photographer's nostrils.

Two views on the quay at Mistley, looking west, August 1905 (above) and 1903. The group of buildings in the centre of the later view form the rear of the Grape Vine inn. Mistley was part of the largest malting district in Essex and the maltings at the far end of the quay had benefited from the partnership between maltster Robert Free and a local ironfounder, who between them had patented mechanical improvements in the handling, grading, drying and sacking parts of the manufacture in the last quarter of the nineteenth century. The malting and kilns have been replaced by modern warehouses, and only a single isolated part of the railway siding remains, embedded in concrete.

Farm worker and two-horse team, near Mistley, July 1899. Although there were concentrations of industry in the principal towns, Essex remained a predominantly agricultural county at the end of the nineteenth century.

Cottage, Mistley, June 1902. This is one of the better type of cottage put up towards the end of the century, seen here with the owner and his dog. Doubtless there would have been an earth closet at the back and cooking on the range, while living conditions would have been cramped as families tended to be large.

Two views of Mistley Fair, the Green, August 1903 (above) and 1907. After the harvest was in, the routine of life at Mistley seems to have been broken by an annual fair in August. The 'talking animated pictures' of latest events may have used film, but are more likely to have been a circus act.

A village wedding party, Bradfield, 1907. Bradfield is a small village south-east of Mistley. Wire had his camera to hand and was looking north up the village street when this wedding party came from the church on the right. Today only the houses with the advert for Saunder's bakery and the cottages in the distance on the bend in the road survive.

AROUND CLACTON
AND HARWICH

The Pier, Clacton-on-Sea, looking from the balcony end and showing the Royal Hotel and the town, August 1904. Clacton owes its existence to Peter Schuyler Bruff, an engineer who worked for the Tendring Hundred Railway Company, and who in 1865 acquired land that now forms the centre of the modern town. He laid out streets, and built a pier in 1871 and the principal hotel. Clacton's pier was extended in 1877. The Pavilion, on whose balcony Wire was standing when he took this photograph, was added in 1893 and provided holiday-makers with shows and concerts over the years. A selection of penny amusement machines are just visible at the bottom left. A member of the pier staff is lighting a gas lamp, suggesting that this was an early evening view.

The Royal Hotel, Clacton-on-Sea, 1904. This hotel was finished in 1872 by Bruff and was later enlarged. There seems to be something of a tête-á-tête going on, oblivious to the camera.

What we came here for – the sands and the cliffs at Clacton-on-Sea, 1904. By this time the tents had replaced wheeled bathing huts as places to change.

The Town Hall, Clacton-on-Sea, 1905. The Town Hall complex, which opened in January 1895, included a bank, shops and an operatic hall. Opera later gave way to films and, still later, to bingo. The Town Hall was to lose its splendid clock tower in a bombing raid in 1941.

St Osyth's Priory, August 1907. The Priory had been established shortly before 1127. Abbot John Vintoner built a mansion adjoining the Priory in the early sixteenth century and the window in the top view formed part of this work, though the building behind was rebuilt in 1865. The bottom photograph shows the fifteenth-century gatehouse.

Two views of the Peoples' Palace camp, Frinton, July 1895. The People's Palace Technical School, situated on the Mile End Road, organized a summer camp for some 230 boys and masters. The chosen destination was Frinton, where the party arrived on 13 July for a nine day holiday. The site had been provided for free by a local landowner, conveniently close to the railway. The party set about erecting twenty-four bell tents, one square tent and a large marquee. The camp had its own post office, depository and lending library. The top view shows the cooks' tent; the bottom view shows one of the bell tents. Wire's son Arthur was treasurer, and these may be his photographs. Curious locals flocked to the camp, and there were expeditions to local beauty spots, yachting trips and a cricket match.

Two views of the People's Palace camp, Frinton, July 1897. This year the week finished with a geological expedition to the well known cliffs at Walton on the Naze, athletic sports and evening entertainments, which included women guests. The top view shows five masters; the bottom view shows the laborious process of packing up the tents onto wagons.

Old houses opposite the church, Dovercourt, August 1908. Modern Dovercourt is effectively a suburb of Harwich, but Dovercourt is the older of the two, for it is mentioned in Domesday, and Harwich was not founded until the twelfth century. The nucleus of the old village of Dovercourt was round the church, which faced these houses. The nearest building has since been replaced by a 1920s house and the furthest forms part of a school. The monumental mason's little shop has been rebuilt in a similar style, and now houses an undertakers.

Dovercourt High Street, in August 1908, looking back towards Kingsway. The shops on the left remain, though they no longer house Hunters' boot and clothing store. Beyond is the Queens Hotel. This was the shopping centre for the town, as indicated by the bustle of local people.

At the top end of Kingsway, Dovercourt, facing out across the Upper Parade towards the sea is the Alexandra Hotel, still comparatively new in August 1904. The buildings beyond have all been replaced and the hotel is now a Methodist Home for the Aged.

The Lower Parade, Dovercourt, August 1908. The growth of Dovercourt owes much to John Bagshaw MP, who died a bankrupt in 1870. His work included the layout of the Upper and Lower Parades. The statue of Queen Victoria, visible in the centre, still presides over the Upper Parade.

The High Lighthouse, Harwich, October 1897. Harwich was created shortly before 1196 by Roger Bigod, Earl of Norfolk, and it was an important sea port in late medieval times. It received a boost in the 1660s with the creation of a royal dockyard, and increased in prosperity in the eighteenth century when good communications with Germany gained in importance under the Hanoverian dynasty. The rebuilt High Lighthouse of 1817 was designed by John Rennie at the same time as its partner, the Low Lighthouse, and is over 70 feet high. Originally it was owned by General Francis Rebow, who made a fortune from charges of 1*d* per ton on all incoming cargoes. The original light was halfway up the tower, but the lighthouse was later modified. Anticipating changes to the channel, Rebow sold the High Lighthouse to Trinity House in 1836, but it was another twenty-seven years before both lighthouses became redundant. The High Lighthouse remained an important landmark to seamen and in 1909 was bought by the borough council.

West Street, Harwich, looking towards the Quay from near the junction with Church Street, August 1907. Near here, a fountain in black-and-white marble was erected that same year, replacing an earlier standpipe and lasting until 1946. In the middle distance, Golden Lion Lane and Church Lane mark the medieval limits of the town.

The east side of West Street, Harwich, 1897, giving a closer view of some of the houses. Georgian prosperity led to some refronting of earlier timber-framed buildings, but not here. Harwich was a depressed area in the 1920s and many buildings were allowed to deteriorate. Much of Church Lane was cleared in 1938 and this part of West Street has also changed.

Church Street, Harwich, looking south towards St Nicholas Church, October 1897. The gabled building to the left is a fifteenth-century timber-framed and plastered house of three bays. Two were demolished in the 1920s for the Wheatsheaf public house. St Nicholas Church dates from 1821, replacing a much altered and repaired original that projected further into the street than its successor. The present church is built of London brick and the artificial Coade stone. Adjoining the church is the Three Cups Hotel, an early sixteenth-century building with seventeenth-century additions. Nelson stayed here with Lady Hamilton. The hotel lost its top storey and had a new front added in 1949.

The Picr Hotel, Harwich, August 1908. The Pier Hotel and the early nineteenth-century Angel inn, on the left, are here seen from Corporation or Ha'penny Pier. This pier was built in 1851–4 and its name refers to the entrance fee. The sheds to the left form part of the shipyard and are the only buildings in this photograph to have been replaced. Just to the right of the Pier Hotel stands the massive Great Eastern Hotel of 1864, which was intended for continental travellers who came in via the railway line, opened in 1854, to catch the steamers from Railway Pier. These arrangements changed with the construction of Parkstone Quay in 1883. After a period as council offices, the hotel has now been converted to flats.

Two views of Thorpe Le Soken, June 1912. Thorpe Le Soken lies on the crossroads of the roads between Harwich and Clacton and between Colchester and Walton on the Naze. The fishing and farming community was once able to support ten public houses, though only five survive today. The top view is looking towards the Crown Hotel; the bottom view is looking towards the Bell Hotel. A hay wagon is passing through the almost deserted street with only the odd delivery cart and pedestrian in view. The shop opposite the Bell Hotel proclaims the latest troubles in the Balkans on its newspaper boards.

CHELMSFORD AND ENVIRONS

The southern end of the High Street with the conduit, Chelmsford, April 1893. Chelmsford gained its bridges over the rivers Can and Chelmer and its market from the bishops of London, who were the medieval lords of the manor. These advantages enabled it to become the principal county town. The railway reached Chelmsford in 1839, but major industrial growth did not begin until the later part of the nineteenth century. The town had gained its charter in 1888, but its principal church was not to become a cathedral until 1914. The conduit was built in 1814 in Tindall Square, replacing an earlier structure with a naiad. The lady survived the demolition and was recovered many years later, chipped and damaged, from a builder's yard. The new conduit was moved to its High Street location in 1851, but even then there was some question as to whether the new site would prove a problem to traffic. In the event it was moved again to its present location in Tower Gardens, not without considerable resistance, in 1940. Wire took this photograph in the late afternoon, when the friends of the conduit obligingly provided a human centrepiece round it.

Edmund Durrant's book and music shop, 90 High Street, Chelmsford, July 1891. This shop stood on the site of the former Three Tuns inn. The adjoining shops shown here are those of J.A. Smith, draper, at No. 89 and the hat shop of William and Edward Davis. Edmund Durrant had been an advocate of the secret ballot in municipal affairs and served on the borough council after incorporation in 1888. He was interested in the history of Chelmsford and in 1908 he published reminiscences with accompanying views. He was present when the cannon was installed outside Shire Hall in 1858, and remembered men in the uniforms of volunteers of 1815 who took part in the ceremony. Wire was probably both customer and friend, and would have keenly supported the newly published guide to Essex.

Two views of the Stone Bridge, Chelmsford, April 1893 and June 1906. The top view is looking from the new Iron Bridge of 1890, and includes a curious windmill used to pump water up from the river for garden use. J.A. Vickridge's main shop was at 53 High Street. The Stone Bridge was the work of county surveyor John Johnson and was completed in 1786. To achieve his graceful single span, Johnson reduced the width of the river from 54 feet to 36 feet, and this was to be a contributory factor to later flooding, which was not remedied until the substantial concrete works of 1962. A former inn called the Cock stood on the far side of the bridge beyond Vickridge's building, which was already disused by 1893. The bottom view shows how the inn was replaced by the Wesleyan Methodist Church and its school of 1898.

Moulsham Street, Chelmsford, looking towards the Stone Bridge and the Methodist Church, June 1906. In the foreground is the Cross Keys inn, which after some years out of use was demolished in 1916 to make way for the Regent Theatre. Two doors down is Rankins, another drapers shop.

The Shire Hall and Tindall Square, Chelmsford, July 1891. The former Russian 36-pounder is to the fore. The foundation stone for the Shire Hall was laid in August 1789, the architect being John Johnson, after his family firm won the contract. Coins and medals from the reign of King George III were buried at the foundation stone laying ceremony, and the workmen were given ten guineas to share between them. The new building included two handsome courtrooms, a ballroom, a market hall and corn exchange.

Museum Terrace, Chelmsford, April 1893. Museum Terrace had been built just less than fifty years before on the west side of New Bridge Street by the printer George Meggy, who was also the editor of the *Chelmsford Chronicle*. The elegant classical range included large private houses, shops, an office and a museum. Meggy founded the Chelmsford Philosophical Society in 1828 and saw the development as providing a home for the society's collection of books, objects and scientific instruments. By 1848 the terrace also included a private school. This row was cleared in postwar redevelopment.

St Mary's Church, Little Baddow, September 1893. Little Baddow lies just to the east of Chelmsford, south of the River Chelmer. Wire had first come here as a young qualified teacher in 1862, and returned, camera in hand, some thirty years later. St Mary's Church has an altered Norman nave – only the north wall and a fifteenth-century chancel remain. The tower was adapted in the fourteenth century. There was an eighteenth-century gallery in Wire's time, which covered a fine wall-painting, discovered when the gallery was removed in 1928.

St Mary's Church and hall, Little Baddow, July 1894. Adjoining the church is Little Baddow Hall, a timber-framed house dating from the fourteenth century. The house beside the churchyard was built for the parish clerk in 1620.

The Rodney, Little Baddow, July 1894. After a long stroll, The Rodney could offer refreshments, and Wire moved on here after his visit to the church. Built on the site of a building called the Warren House, which dated from before 1620, the Rodney was previously a tavern, known as the Cock and Warren in 1777. It was renamed in the late eighteenth century. In 1885 Elizabeth Mecklenburg opened a pleasure garden here, which became a popular venue for church outings.

Little Baddow National School and the schoolmaster's house, September 1893. The first school in the parish had been founded in 1532, and this merged with a charity school in 1836. The new schoolroom seen here was completed in 1851. From 1850 the schoolmaster was also the village postman, and after his death his wife, Susan Horth, continued to run the school, assisted by a succession of teachers, of whom Wire was one. The log book suggests that Wire was in charge! After 1866 the school was taken over by Susan Horth's third son and was enlarged in 1896 to cope with additional infants. Later accounts recall the open fires in winter, lit in rotation by pupils, while inspectors' reports speak of poor ventilation – not the best atmosphere for learning.

The Bell inn and neighbouring houses, Willingale Doe, July 1912. This inn faced the churchyard of the two Willingale parish churches, with St Christopher's Church to the north serving Willingale Doe and St Andrew's Church ministering to Willingale Spain. Both churches were combined into a single parish in 1929. The Bell has ceased to be a public house within the last ten years, and the two houses to the north have now gone, together with the barn at the rear. The beech on the left was a casualty of the 1987 storm.

WALTHAM ABBEY, EPPING AND DISTRICT

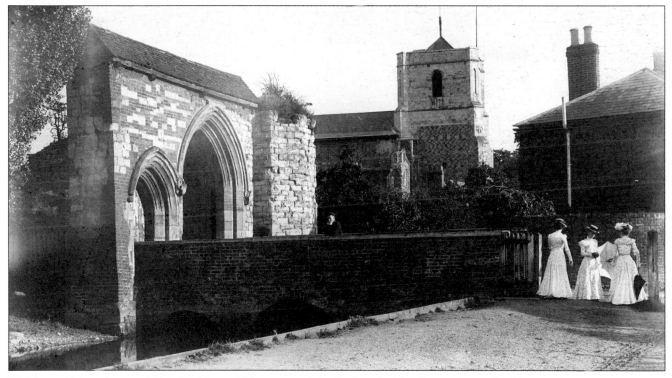

Waltham Abbey, August 1901. Waltham Abbey was originally founded by Canute's standard bearer, but was rebuilt and re-endowed by Harold, then Saxon Earl of Essex, who went on to gain the throne, only to lose it at the Battle of Hastings in 1066. Subsequently it became an Augustinian house in 1177, then seven years later a 'mitred abbey', going on to become one of the wealthiest houses in England. During the Dissolution of the Monasteries, much was swept away, and only part of the nave survived to serve as the parish church. This photograph was taken from the bridge by the Abbey Gateway, both of which date from the fourteenth century. The church had a new tower built after 1559, when the original one collapsed. The new tower was without its top part for twenty years after 1778, then underwent restoration in 1905, producing its present appearance. The church roof was lowered in 1808. Some of Wire's family are posing in their summer dresses in front of a cottage that now no longer remains. Trees have grown up in front of the church so that it is now almost obscured from the bridge in summer.

The Welsh Harp, Waltham Abbey, 6 September 1902. This fifteenth-century inn incorporates a lychgate to the abbey, and may once have formed part of the abbey buildings. Today, beams have been exposed on the upper floor, while weatherboarding in the area by the little gate and the gate itself have gone.

High Bridge Street, Waltham Abbey, August 1901, with the abbey church tower. Wire took this photograph while standing near the river bridge. The shops on the right were demolished in 1902 to make way for the construction of the present Waltham Holy Cross council building and the adjacent shops.

Church Street, Waltham Abbey, September 1902. The post office in Market Square is just visible from Church Street. Edward Lawrence's hairdressing saloon, opposite the east end of the churchyard, still retains its plastering, though it no longer caters for the hirsute. The house closer to the square has lost its weatherboarding and gained a new window.

The Market Square, Waltham Abbey, looking towards the Sun Street junction, June 1906, when John Ives was the postmaster. The corner house is no longer the post office and its rendering has changed, but it and the adjoining houses all survive. The buildings on the opposite side of the street have given way to a modern bank, apart from the house with the tall chimneys.

Waltham Abbey's main livestock market was in Romeland, to the north of Church Street, seen here in June 1906. The name probably refers to the wasteland that existed before the market was created. In 1876 it was noted that the narrow and crooked streets were lined with poor houses, and slum clearance was to begin in 1892.

The eastern side of Romeland, Waltham Abbey, June 1906. The Crown public house is on the corner and is the only surviving building today, for the rest of Romeland is now occupied by modern brick and weatherboarded council houses. The lamp in front of the houses in the background tops a drinking fountain that brought up water from 168 feet below. It was paid for by public subscription in May 1878. It still survives, with some surrounding cobbles, but perhaps someone should consider restoring the lamp standard.

To the south-east of Waltham Abbey lies Honey Lane Vale. In this view, of August 1901, the thatched cattle trough is in poor repair. The house on the corner of Woodgreen Road has since been replaced and the field around the trough is now a car park.

The bridge on Claypit Hill, looking north to the junction with Honey Lane, Waltham Abbey, August 1901. The fencing of the Volunteer public house is on the left. During the ninety years since this photograph was taken, alterations to the road and greatly increased hedging have altered this scene almost beyond recognition.

The Volunteer public house, Honey Lane Vale, Waltham Abbey, August 1900. Both the public house and the barn have been rebuilt.

Mott Lane, High Beech, Waltham Abbey, 1904. Wire was possibly looking east when he took this photograph. Although the road has been made up and small tiled outhouses are less in evidence, Mott Street (as it is now) still remains quiet and tree-lined.

Forest Lodge, Waltham Abbey, August 1901. Wire described this house and its refreshment room as 'Forest Lodge, Honey Lane Vale', but it is more likely to be the Forest Lodge that was situated to the north of the lane in Upshire. There were three tea rooms in this area of Epping Forest alone that had sprung up to cater for cyclists and horse brake parties from London.

Abridge, 1898. Abridge is situated on the road from Loughton to Chelmsford. This is now the Market Place, near the site of the present roundabout. The two houses on the right survive, but that nearer to the camera has lost its weatherboarding and has a new shopfront. Rigg's Retreats provided refreshments in the Epping Forest area at the end of the nineteenth century, and the Abridge establishment was just one of their properties. The houses in the distance were to become a restaurant by 1915, kept by Mrs G. Brightly, and known locally as Old Mother Brightly's.

David Livingstone's cottage, Chipping Ongar, May 1913. Richard Cecil, minister of the Nonconformist church at Chipping Ongar, ran a small training school for missionaries from 1828 to 1847. One student in 1838/9 was the young David Livingstone, and the inscription above the door recalls his stay here.

The High Street, Chipping Ongar, looking south from the Kings Head public house (right), 5 March 1893, showing the back of the old Town Hall. This had once included a pound as well as the cage for prisoners and held accommodation for local paupers in 1844. In the later part of 1896 it was sold, and by 1897 it had been demolished. The town's hiring fair was revived in 1872 and held in the Town Hall, to help the different classes to mix together. Others thought differently, however, and it was abolished for good in 1892. Many of the buildings shown here survive, including the shop on the right, now an Indian restaurant.

Chigwell Grammar School, June 1898. This school was one of two founded by Samuel Harsnett, who had been vicar of Chigwell from 1597 to 1605 and went on to become Archbishop of York. The grammar school dates from 1629 and the visiting party are looking at the one of the original buildings. William Penn, the founder of Pennsylvania, was a pupil here and would have been taught in this building. The school was enlarged in 1775 and again in the 1860s, when boarding houses were acquired in the village. Grants from Essex County Council in the year that Wire took this photograph enabled considerable improvements to be made in the teaching of science, which would have met with his hearty approval.

Two views of the King's Head public house, Chigwell, July 1895 and May 1907. This inn features in Charles Dickens' *Barnaby Rudge* as The Maypole and courts for Epping Forest met here. It was also a place of feasting, with pigeon pie a house speciality. The top view shows what may be some of Wire's family in the distance; the bottom view shows the alterations of 1901, when an additional bay was added to the upper floor at the far end, together with an addition.

The Wake Arms near Loughton, Epping, June 1912. This was a late addition to the several public houses of Epping, dating from after 1897. It appears to have succeeded in attracting passing motor trade. The man on the right is admiring a very new motor tricycle. Today the inn's successor adjoins the modern Wake Arms roundabout.

Woodlands, Bury Street, Epping, May 1893. This was the home of Mr C.B. Sworder, a local corn and seed merchant, so it is likely that those present include members of his family.

Epping Street and St John's Church, July 1891. St John's Church replaced the earlier Chapel of Ease in 1888–9 and is seen here without its present-day tower, which was added in 1907. The trees along the street were planted as part of the 1887 Jubilee celebrations.

The joys of summer. Donkey riding at an unknown location in Epping Forest, August 1901.

Latton Priory, May 1893. This priory was one of those monastic foundations that justified the dissolution. For many years it had supported just one prior and two canons, but by 1534 even the surviving canon had gone and the visiting commissioners found it had become 'a profane place'. Only one building survived the dissolution, and this was used for many years as a barn (centre).

Two views of Hill House, Theydon Mount, August 1895. The splendid Hill House was the seat of the lords of the manor of Theydon from the sixteenth century to the late nineteenth century. The house was the creation of Sir Thomas Smyth, who served as ambassador to France in 1562. Work began between 1557 and 1560, but was not finished when Smyth died in 1577, for his will included further instructions to the architect, Richard Kirkby. The house was much altered in later centuries, gaining sash windows and the pediment on the east front (above), though it is possible that the columns might be Elizabethan – if so, this would make them a unique feature for this period. Hill House was on the market at the time of Wire's visit and was shortly to be the home of an eccentric who called himself the Duke de Moro. The photograph below shows the south front.

The entrance hall, Hill House. The paintings may have been arranged for Wire's benefit, or his visit may have taken place while the old owners were moving out – or the new one in. The house was to undergo considerable internal alterations at the hands of a later owner from 1912 onwards. Following bomb damaged in 1940, the house was restored in 1950–2, when sixteenth-century wall-paintings were discovered. Shortly afterwards, Hill House was taken over for use as an open women's prison, and this is how it remains today. The magnificent bed on the left is claimed to be sixteenth century.

St Andrew's Church from the south-east, Greensted-juxta-Ongar, March 1893. Apart from the clearance of ivy from the chancel and changes in churchyard planting, this could almost be a modern view. The form of the nave with its logs dates from about 845, though the logs were plastered over prior to restorations by Philip Ray in 1837. The original logs were rotten, so they were shortened and put onto a brick base. The windows in the Tudor tiled roof also date from the restoration.

BETWEEN THE
THAMES AND THE
CROUCH

Canvey Island post office and thatched well, August 1910. Canvey Island owes the well to the efforts of the Revd Henry Hayes, who organized a public subscription, topped up with money from the Corporation of London. The well was put up at the junction of Long Road and Haven Road, and was opened with due ceremony and water sampling on 5 December 1889. Just to the left is the Old Red Cow inn, which, rebuilt and renamed the King Canute after the floods of 1953, still stands. The well was dismantled for road improvements and even the plaque marking the site has now been moved to the Dutch Cottage Museum.

A view between Benfleet and Canvey Island, July 1904. Before the construction of the present-day bridge in 1931, the only way across to the island was by ferry, one of which can be seen in this photograph.

Wash day at the Lobster Smack, Haven Road, Canvey Island, August 1910. Much of Canvey Island was reclaimed from the sea with the help of a Dutchman, Joas Croppenbur, in the seventeenth century. It must have been thirsty work, and no doubt ale would have been welcome to the workers. This public house has been called the Sluice House, and, appropriately, World's End. A roof tile is dated 1510, but the building is probably seventeenth century. It was once a venue for Dutch fishermen, smugglers and prize fights. The Lobster Smack is still serving today.

Southend-by-the-Sea, August 1898. Southend was originally no more than a lane to the sea in the parish of Prittlewell, becoming a place for sea bathing at the end of the eighteenth century. A new town was begun in the 1790s and the first pier was built in 1830. This is the second of Southend's loading piers, built shortly after the second passenger pier in 1891, but it was soon found to be incapable of handling all the potential traffic and was replaced in 1913–14.

Southend, looking west from the passenger pier, August 1910. Top right is Southend Terrace, whose first house was completed in 1792. The coming of the railway in 1856 greatly increased Southend's popularity and by 1911 its population had reached 67,700. In 1906 locals even proposed that it should change its name to Thamesmouth as a sign of its new status. More visitors meant more amenities, and the Pier Hill Buildings were part of this trend, built in 1898. The development included seawater baths, restaurants, shelters, shops, a photographic studio and a reading room. After remaining empty and derelict for some years, the site was cleared in 1977.

Southend, 11 June 1910, looking east from the pier. The dome of the Kursaal amusement centre is just visible in the distance. Some of the buildings in this view survive today, including the gabled arcade, the Ivy Hotel (just discernible with its distinctive pair of bays) and the Hope Hotel, but blinds have all given way to brashly lit amusement arcades and games machines.

Southend-by-the-Sea, August 1898. Wire took this photograph from a little further west. The old loading pier with its cranes can just be seen in the distance, while boys are getting ready to paddle in the foreground. Zanchi's Tearooms have long passed into history, but the distinctive bow-windowed terrace still survives, though the horizon is no longer graced with the gas tower.

Queen Victoria is pointing regally out to sea from her pedestal at the top of Pier Hill, and horse cabs queue patiently for trade behind her. The statue was presented to the town to celebrate the Diamond Jubilee of 1897. This photograph was probably taken a year later. The Queen's statue was to prove an obstacle to traffic and was moved to its current position on Clifftown Parade in 1962.

The Palace Hotel, Southend-by-the-Sea, June 1905. Susan Wire provides the foreground to the view of this new hotel, seen from Southend Pier. Built as the Metropole Hotel on Pier Hill, it opened on Whit Monday 1904, with a band and 500 invited guests, who had over two hundred rooms to choose from and could take advantage of a billiard room and the elaborately decorated bar. The hotel was in use as a military hospital during the First World War. Today its lower reaches are clogged with rather tacky amusement arcades. The pier has been damaged by three fires in its history, the most recent one in June 1995, on the last day spent researching this book. The bowling alley situated at the landward end of the pier (on the site of the low building) was destroyed and the pier end was badly damaged.

Wire described this view as showing the Ivy House, Leigh-on-Sea, August 1910. This house stood at the southern end of what was later named Elm Road and was originally called Black House. Built in about 1600, it was refronted in the mid-nineteenth century by its owner, David Montague, who owned a local pottery and brickworks. Two years after Wire took this photograph the house changed hands and the new owner cleared away the encroaching ivy. It was demolished for the construction of Broadway West in 1927.

The esplanade, Westcliff, August 1910. The promenade and sea walls at Westcliff were constructed between 1903 and 1906. Wire took this photograph while standing with his back to the end of the works. The Palmiera Towers Hotel (right), which was built just before 1903, survived until 1978.

East Street, Prittlewell, August 1910. At this time East Street formed one of the routes to the seafront at Southend, and the public houses and shops would have hoped to do well from passing trade. The Spread Eagle inn, in the foreground, was first recorded in 1784. It was the departure point for the London carrier in 1848, before the coming of the railway.

East Street, Prittlewell, looking towards the junction with North and West Streets, August 1910. Beyond the weatherboarded Deeds Cottages, later nineteenth-century terraces have recently been built. The little market village was soon to be swallowed up in housing estates in the first three decades of the twentieth century. Deeds Cottages and the adjoining shop – later Ye Olde Prittlewell Bakery – were demolished for road improvements in the 1950s. North Street is now incorporated into Victoria Avenue and old Prittlewell has been almost buried as a mere suburb of Southend.

The Martyrs Memorial, Rayleigh, was put up in 1908 as a memorial to Thomas Causton and John Ardeley, two Protestant victims of the Marian Bishop Bonner, who were burnt here in 1556. Wire's photograph of August 1910 has also captured the ornate village pump and an empty milk churn awaiting collection. The memorial still stands, but the house on the right and the fountain have gone.

Rayleigh was once a village of some 5,000 people, and this view of August 1910 captures much of the village peace. The tower of Holy Trinity Church at the end of the street dates from the fifteenth century. Rayleigh was a popular place for private schools, and as late as 1895 there was a finishing school for girls kept by Miss Abbott in a house on the High Street, close to the church.

Two views of the High Street, Rayleigh, July 1908. The top view is looking south and shows the houses in the previous photograph. The fountain is in place and the area adjacent has been fenced off, ready for the construction of the Martyrs Memorial. Rayleigh had its own carnival from 1900 to 1957, and the High Street was also the venue for an annual horse fair, which lasted until 1919. The trees were planted in 1900. Some of the buildings shown still survive, including the drapers shop in a fourteenth-century timber-framed building. In the bottom view, most of the buildings have made way for modern shops.

The tower of St Nicholas Church from the west, Canewdon, August 1910. This parish church stands close to the summit of Beacon Hill. The tower dates from the fifteenth century. The small wooden building on the left was the parish lock-up, which dated from 1775 and housed the parish stocks. Today there are more trees and bushes in the churchyard, and the lock-up and cottage have vanished as if they had never existed.

Eastlands Farm, Bradwell-on-Sea, August 1907. This farmhouse lies on the Roman road running east of the village of Bradwell on the way to the Roman fort. Wire stopped off here on his way to visit St Peter's Church. The tenant farmer was James Brown, who had come down from Northumberland 'to test the excellence of Essex soil', and was just one of many farmers who came to take the place of those who had gone under in the agricultural depression. In 1852 69 acres of land reclaimed from the sea were added to the farm. The marshes made an ideal landing place for smugglers, and the last instance of traditional smuggling of spirits took place in 1854.

St Peter's on the Walls, Bradwell-on-Sea, September 1907. Christianity in Essex owed much to St Cedd, who reached the county from Northumberland in 654. One of his two foundations was at Othona, a Roman seafort, where this church was built over the ruined Roman walls. Later to become St Peter's on the Walls, it was downgraded to a barn for many years. The porch and barn door were removed in subsequent restorations.

St Peter's on the Walls, Bradwell-on-Sea, September 1907. This interior view of St Peter's shows the west wall, and a fine array of wheelbarrows and rural junk.

St Mary's Church porch, Burnham-on-Crouch, July 1889. An advance party of the Essex Field
Club, including their honorary librarian, Alfred Wire, have arrived at the south porch of the church
and have paused under the heraldic shields 'to allow Mr Wire to take some photographs', their
secretary recorded. The primary purpose of the expedition was a nature trip to Foulness Island and
Maplin Sands, but antiquities were also included. Their host for the guided tour of the church was
the Rector of Southminster, Revd G.C. Berkeley. The main party was to join this group shortly
afterwards.

Hill House, Burnham-on-Crouch, July 1889. From the church the advance guard sped to the railway station, to meet the main party. Then the whole party retraced their steps to Hill House, on the north side of the lane to Althorne, where their hosts, Mr and Mrs John Rogers, had pitched a marquee on the lawn and laid out a splendid lunch. The president, Mr Fitch, thanked Mr Rogers for the lunch and for his part in arranging access to coastal areas usually closed by the military. And everyone assembled for Wire to take this photograph. Hill House was demolished in 1967.

One of the manors of Benfleet was Jarvis Hall at Thundersley. This view of April 1908 shows the old barn, just off Kiln Road below Bread and Cheese Hill (both now part of Thundersley Park Road). It had once been a medieval house and was reputed to be a hunting lodge built by King John.

Highfield House, Thundersley, 1908. Thundersley was a very retired place at the time, so much so that Mrs C. Post had decided it would make the perfect spot for her Voluntary Retreat for Male Inebriates, presumably at some distance from the owners of Highfield House.

The Railway Hotel, Southminster, September 1901. This hotel was comparatively new when Wire took this photograph. It was built in anticipation of trade from the branch of the Great Eastern Railway that terminated here. Seven years later the licensee was C. Downing.

Stanford-Le-Hope parish church from the west, August 1903. This church, dedicated to St Margaret of Antioch, is dominated by its tower of 1883. The west front is of similar date, but the core is older. The rebuilding of the church reflected the change of the settlement from village to small town.

By contrast, St Mary's Church, Corringham, retains its early Norman tower. The open niche serves as one of the bell openings. The remainder of the church dates from the fourteenth century and when Alfred photographed it in August 1903 it was the centre of a small and isolated village on the edge of the marshes.

BRENTWOOD AND BASILDON

The north side of the High Street, Brentwood, March 1913. Brentwood's name commemorates a late twelfth-century clearance of woodland. The High Street was built up by 1788 and although the railway arrived in 1839, major development did not begin until the 1880s. At the time of Wire's visit, a major estate at Warley was still under construction, and the High Street remained a mixture of buildings dating from three centuries. Change was under way, as this view shows, looking east from near the Lion and Lamb public house. Brentwood Palace cinema was finished in 1914, rebuilt in 1934 and closed in 1968.

The High Street, Brentwood, looking east, March 1913. The children are lingering by Kelso's bakery on the north side of the High Street. In the middle distance is the eighteenth-century Swan inn, which was rebuilt in 1935.

The High Street, Brentwood, looking west, March 1913. The Lion and Lamb Hotel may well be linked to an inn that, in 1581, was called the Lamb, though the 1913 building was the result of a rebuild after a fire. This was the public house used by the local Liberal Party in mid-Victorian years.

The High Street, Brentwood, looking west, October 1903. Behind the splendid carriage are the shops of Paul & Sons, ironmongers, and Wilson and Whitworths, printers.

The High Street, Brentwood, looking east, October 1903. This view shows the White Hart public house, dating from the early sixteenth century. Extended and altered in the nineteenth century, the inn was the local Conservative stronghold. In 1874 the Liberals hired a German band and had it march past the White Hart, and a fight ensued. The public house was substantially rebuilt in the 1930s.

Brentwood Grammar School and the Martyrs Oak in 1903. Alfred's view includes the oldest part of the school, founded in 1558 by Sir Antony Browne, Lord Chief Justice, and the school chapel.

Bentley Mill, Bentley Common, June 1905. David John Morgan (1844–1918) was the MP for the Walthamstow division of Essex from 1900 to 1906, but his home was Bentley Mill. This suggests that it had replaced the post mill, which stood on the north-east side of Mores Lane until it was dismantled in 1884. Morgan has posed for Wire outside the garden front of his ivy-covered house. Today it is called Cedar House, and it is comparatively unchanged.

The old Rectory, South Ockenden, 1910. This house stood a little south of the village of South Ockenden on the west side of South Road. It dated back to 1610, but had nineteenth-century additions and had once been moated. It was bought by London County Council in 1952 with glebe land, then later demolished for a housing estate, which was built in about 1970.

The High Street, South Ockenden, 1910. The main road from Brentwood to Thurrock ran through South Ockenden village. A station was opened to the west of the village in 1892, but it had little effect on the population, which rose by fewer than 100 from the 1861 total of 1,267 people in the succeeding seventy years. Radical change did not come until the later 1930s with the construction of the London County Council estate in neighbouring Aveley. Alfred Poulter the grocer was still trading in 1929, but his shop had changed hands by 1933.

Aveley village, 1897. Aveley originated as a large village on rising ground north of the River Mardyke. It grew little in the nineteenth century, and in 1901 the population was a mere 1,060. This view shows a mixture of timber-framed and nineteenth-century brick buildings. A large part of the parish was taken up with the Belhus estate, until it was sold off for the construction of the LCC estate. Change then followed rapidly, and the majority of the older houses in the village were to be demolished in the nine years after 1945.

Belhus, just outside Aveley, June 1897. Belhus took its name from a fourteenth-century tenant, but the house was largely the work of John Barrett, who described it as 'newly builded' in his will of 1526. It was owned by the Barrett-Lennard family until 1919, when the sale of the estate opened up the Aveley area for development. Much of the park was included in the green belt, but the house, damaged by bombs in the Second World War, was demolished in 1957. Some architectural features survive in Thurrock Museum.

Grays–Thurrock railway cutting, between Grays and Upminster, July 1890. Most railways in Essex were constructed before the age of photography, but there were some later additions, including a branch from Grays to Romford, built by the Great Eastern Railway. The first part, from Grays to Upminster, was opened in 1892. This view from the south shows work in progress on the first bridge from Thurrock.

Oliphants Manor House, Basildon, October 1913. It was recorded on the site in 1484, and the strange name was derived from a thirteenth-century owner, Juliana Honeyward, or her successor, Henry de Uniwent. Local pronunciation made this 'Onyfaunt', 'Allyvants' and even the homely 'Elephants' at various times. The house was a three-gabled timber-framed building and was destroyed in a fire in 1902. This building replaced it and became the rectory in the 1930s. It was badly damaged by bombs in 1940 and by a V-2 in 1945. It was finally demolished when the Ford Tractor Plant was constructed.

Upminster Hall, July 1890. This was one of the manors given by King Harold to his newly founded abbey at Waltham Holy Cross, a gift confirmed in 1062. After the Dissolution of the Monasteries in 1534, Upminster Hall passed to Thomas Cromwell, but was reclaimed by the Crown in 1540. The Latham family owned it from 1549 to 1642, after which it passed to the Noel family, who sold it in 1686 to Andrew Branfill, a master mariner of Stepney. The Branfill family retained the estate, which ran to 674 acres in the nineteenth century, until 1906. Much of it was developed in the 1900s, but the house and its surrounds were leased to the Upminster Golf Club, which bought the freehold in 1935. The hall is mainly sixteenth century, though parts may date back to its days as an abbey farm. The distant wing (left) is an eighteenth-century addition. Later additions have been made since 1935.

St Lawrence Church and part of the rectory, from the meadows, Upminster, 1904. The tower of this church dates from about 1200 and the framing of the spire from later in the century, but the rest of the church was rebuilt in 1862. The rectory was constructed in 1740, replacing a ruinous predecessor. By this date the tithe barn to the west of the rectory had already been demolished, though it had served as a place of worship while the church was being reconstructed.

HAVERING, BARKING
AND DAGENHAM

Wennington Road, Rainham, looking north-west towards the Broadway, April 1909. The village of Rainham would not have been considered as 'London over the border' in Wire's time, though today it forms part of the London borough of Havering. This is the first picture featured here of those areas lost to Essex in 1965. Wire took this photograph while standing not far from the station, which opened in 1854. To the right is the Church of St Helan and St Giles, which dates substantially from the twelfth century. The tower received its buttresses and battlements in the sixteenth century, and the church was still undergoing the last stages of a restoration that had begun in 1897 and was not completed for another year after Wire's visit. Rainham, with its creek to the south, was a dumping place for London night soil and rubbish, and made use of this in market gardening. Major change came after the First World War, when a new suburb grew up around the old village.

The north front of Hare Hall, Gidea Park, 1895, now on the west side of Upper Brentwood Road. It was still a private house at the time of this photograph. The hall was built in 1768–9 by John Wallenger, and the architect was James Pain. This Palladian house had a pavilion on either side, linked to the main block by columned corridors. These were to be filled in by substantial additions in 1896. The house was taken by the Royal Liberty School in 1921, which enlarged on the service ranges at the back to form a quadrangle. Though the landscaped park has been changed, the house with its extensions remains in school use today.

The Rectory, Cranham, May 1904. Cranham was a small agricultural parish just to the north of Upminster, with a population of under 400 in 1901. The Rectory had replaced an earlier one of 1610 on the same site in 1790, using materials from the recently demolished Cranham Hall. Both the rectory and the glebe were sold for development in 1924, and the present-day rectory was built closer to the church.

Church Street, Dagenham, looking east to the church of St Peter and St Paul, June 1904. Dagenham was a small village centred on Crown Street and the church, whose rather strange Gothic tower with its curly battlements dates from about 1800. The coming of the railway did not make a substantial difference to the population here, but the deep anchorage to the south on the River Thames proved attractive to industry, including the Ford Motor Company.

Parsloes, Dagenham, July 1904, took its name from the medieval Passelaw family. It was rebuilt in the sixteenth century and given various additions by the Fanshawe family, who owned the house from 1619 until 1923. The Revd John Fanshawe was responsible for an extensive rebuilding, and he added the battlements and gothic sash windows. The family ceased to live there after 1858, and the house and estate were sold in stages from 1901. Demolition took place in 1925, and the estate was divided between Becontree housing estate and the present-day Parsloes Park.

Whalebone House, Chadwell Heath, March 1899. This is the gateway to the aptly named Whalebone House, formerly Beansland House. The high eighteenth-century front conceals a house that was built in the previous century. As a result of bombing during the Second World War, nothing of it now remains.

Barking Creek and boat yards, April 1893. This creek and its quay had been the landing place for provisions going to Barking Abbey. Later trade included corn and meal to and from the mills, together with hay and reeds from the marshes. The creek also had its own fishing industry, though by the time of this photograph it was in terminal decline. The nineteenth century had seen problems with landing manure and carting it through Barking for the market gardens – a problem alleviated with the decline of shipping in the creek.

Windmill, Chadwell Heath, 1899. This is the last of three windmills, all on the same site at Chadwell Heath. This one was a tribute to the energy of the Archer family, who were active from the 1820s. The mills were called Long Sally, Little Jenny and, this one, Miss Bentley, so called as it had been brought from Bentley Heath in about 1820. Long Sally was destroyed by lightning. Although there was an experiment with electricity in 1882, Miss Bentley was still wind-powered when Wire made a visit here. This mill was to last until 1906.

Wellington Mill, Barking, September 1905. This mill was named after the victor of Waterloo when it was built in 1815. After 1887 the miller was William Firman, who was succeeded by his son John in 1902. Just prior to Wire's visit, two of the sails had blown off during a storm. These do not appear to have been replaced, as a result of which electricity took over. However, the fabric of the mill was allowed to deteriorate and it was finally demolished in 1926.

The Friends Meeting House, Barking, seen here in 1905, dated from the sixteenth century. It had once been a private house called Tates Place, when the local Quakers bought a plot opposite to serve as a burial ground in 1672. They acquired the house in the following year. The community at Barking included several wealthy tradesmen, including William Mead (1628–1713). The meeting house was partly rebuilt in 1758, but the congregation declined in numbers after 1780 and the building was closed in 1830. The house was retained for occasional services and the burial ground remained in use. The most famous interment was Elizabeth Fry, the prison reformer, who died in 1845. With the establishment of a new meeting house in 1891, the old one was no longer adequate and was demolished in 1908. Stone fireplaces, wooden panelling and an elders' bench survive in its successor.

The junction of North Street, East Street and the Broadway, Barking, May 1907. The market stalls are on the Broadway. To the left is the Bull Hotel, which originally dated from the fifteenth century. Pellings the grocers, a boot repairers and Joseph Hart, butcher, are on the other side of the Congregational Church, which was built in 1864. Substantial changes have taken place since this photograph was taken: the Bull Hotel was rebuilt in 1925, William King's shop and the other buildings around the church have all been replaced, and the Congregational Church was demolished in the 1950s.

The old Moot Hall, Barking, July 1893. It was built in the centre of Barking market-place in 1567–8 as the market hall and local courthouse. In the later sixteenth century the ground floor was open to the street and used as a corn market. The upper floors housed the JP's chamber, a small courtroom, the local armoury and a school. The cage for local criminals was still there in the 1890s, and much of the ground floor remained open. The building gradually deteriorated and was pulled down in 1921. Some timbering and panels still survive in the present-day Barking Town Hall.

Little Blake Hall, Wansted, from the garden, July 1893. The house and its estate adjoined Blake Hall, west of George Green. The last tenant kept a fine pack of hounds, which were a local curiosity. The estate is now covered by Draycot, Seagry and part of Felsted Roads.

Cyclists enjoying a leisurely ride along Blake Hall Road, Wanstead, May 1897. The gate on the right leads to Wanstead Park.

REDBRIDGE

St Mary's Church, Wanstead, from the north-west, May 1891. At this time the church had the advantage of open space around it, which has now been taken up with modern buildings. This building is situated 70 feet to the south of the original parish church, which was demolished in 1790 when St Mary's, designed by William Hardwick, was completed. It has been little altered subsequently, and retains its box pews and fine pulpit with a sounding board.

The old George inn and the houses at the bottom of Snaresbrook High Street, Wanstead, 1897. George had once had a Dragon to grapple with in the inn's name, but the saint had long since gained the upper hand in Wanstead and his adversary had departed. The old inn had an engraved cherrystone set in the wall, which commemorated the cheeky theft of a passing cherry pie by a workman from his perch up a ladder in 1752.

The new George inn, Wanstead, 1906. An inn was first recorded here in 1716 and the old building probably dated from that time, but in about 1902 it was pulled down. To the right is Sheridan House, an early eighteenth-century building, once the home of Richard Brinsley Sheridan, the playwright. It was demolished in the 1920s for the construction of Eastern Avenue. George Green became a public space in the late 1870s, and was once a popular place for playing cricket. The chestnut trees were also useful for stringing out laundry lines. The little edifice on George Green is a drinking fountain, erected to commemorate Queen Victoria's Golden Jubilee in 1897. Wire would have approved. Although it has been moved recently, the fountain still exists.

The Broadway, Ilford, July 1905, looking towards the monumental White Horse inn of 1889. This ceased to be a public house in the 1950s and was, until recently, a drapers shop. Dentists seem to have been emboldened at the turn of the century and advertisements for sets of false teeth graced newspapers – however, Mr Richard's commissioned artwork is surely one of the largest examples of the genre.

St Chad's Well, Billet Road, Chadwell Heath, September 1907. This was a popular spot for photographers. The well has long vanished, but a plaque put up in the Festival of Britain year marks the site.

This is the lower of the two principal bridges over the River Roding, seen here in 1905, a year after the earlier brick bridge of 1759–64 had been replaced by a steel, brick and concrete structure. An Act of 1737 permitted barge navigation between Barking Quay and Ilford Bridge, and one vessel is moored by the adjacent yards.

The Red Bridge over the River Roding, Ilford, May 1896. This is the upper of the two bridges over the river. The Red House, now known as the White House, is in the background. The Red Bridge was situated above Wanstead Park, where the river had been divided in the early eighteenth century to feed the lake. This peaceful rural scene was transformed by the construction of Eastern Avenue in the 1920s and of the present-day Red Bridge, which was completed in 1926.

Great Gearies, Cranbrook Road, Barkingside, July 1895. Not long after Wire took this photograph, this eighteenth-century house was demolished and a smaller house built on the site, with only the original gates and railings remaining.

Little Gearies, Cranbrook Road, Barkingside, June 1891. This garden view was taken with what looks like the family in attendance. This house and its grounds were replaced by a council estate in the 1950s.

Two photographs of Gaysham Hall, Barkingside, August 1895. This hall was situated a quarter of a mile to the east of Clayhall and took its name from a late thirteenth-century tenant. It was bought by Thomas Wight in 1607 and remained with his descendants for over two hundred years. The medieval manor house was pulled down before 1716 and this gabled L-shaped farmhouse took its place. The Gaysham estate was sold for building development in 1927, but the house remained standing until 1945, when it fell victim to a V-1. It was demolished in 1947. The site now forms part of the Longwood Gardens estate.

The top view shows the drawing room at Gaysham Hall, which contained fine panelling, while the mirror over the fireplace provides a glimpse back into the room; the bottom view shows the bedroom fireplace, which dated back to the early nineteenth century.

The Eagle inn, Snaresbrook, summer 1912. This was an early eighteenth-century public house, whose nineteenth-century alterations included the balcony, which is visible in this view. This was the occasion of the Woodford Cyclists Meet.

The Woodford Cyclists Meet, the Eagle inn, Snaresbrook, 1904.

Two views of Lake House, Wanstead, January 1908 (above) and September 1906. This house was built within the Wanstead Park estate on an island in the most westerly of the artificial lakes in the early eighteenth century. It may have been intended as a summer residence or a banqueting hall, but was damp, subject to draughts and overrun with rabbits. For three years from 1832, it was home to the poet Thomas Hood, whose son was born here, being hastily baptized in case the damp carried him off. In its later years it was used as a sports pavilion by various local clubs. The top view is looking from from Wanstead Flats, a few months before the house was demolished; the bottom view shows the splendours of the banqueting hall, which included a Grinling Gibbons fireplace and painted wall decorations that depicted the four seasons.

Two views of the Easter Fair, Wanstead Flats, 1903. This fair began at the end of the eighteenth century as a cattle market but became a pleasure fair in the late nineteenth century, eventually ceasing in around 1913. Thurstons were all set to give the twentieth century all the fun they could muster.

NEWHAM

East Ham Town Hall, September 1905. Wire took this photograph two years after the Town Hall had been completed. It was the first of the group of municipal buildings put up on the High Street and Barking Road corner, and was designed by the memorably named partnership of Cheers and Smith.

Two views of Boleyn Castle, East Ham, July and August 1895. Wire appears to have made a couple of visits to Boleyn Castle, which adjoined Green Street. The house was built for Richard Breame (d.1546), and while there was a connection with Ann Boleyn's brother Lord Rochford, there is no evidence that King Henry VIII's second wife ever lived in the house. After passing through various families, the estate was bought by Cardinal Manning for use as a Roman Catholic church and primary school in 1869. Evidence of this can be seen in the photograph below, which shows the doorway. There were later alterations to the house, but the garden tower was original. In the eighteenth century its upper room was hung with gold-embossed leather, but by the late 1890s the house and its small estate were close to a road busy with the clank of trams. After Wire's visit the house became a maternity home and much of the estate was leased to West Ham Football Club. The house was used as a social club before 1939, but was allowed to fall into ruin after the Second World War and was finally demolished in 1955.

The back of Boleyn Castle, and (below) the tower, 1895.

The Spotted Dog public house, Upton, July 1893. This public house still had its own tea garden and cricket ground when Wire took this photograph. Part of the inn dated from the sixteenth century, though it had a large yellow brick extension added in the late nineteenth century. Clapton Football Club, which was formed in 1878, used part of the grounds in 1888, and it was also popular as a venue for school sporting events. This public house is still a popular venue today.

Cottages, West Ham Lane, October 1900. This weatherboarded and brick row of small houses stood on the east side of the lane, opposite the Abbey Schools. The buildings may have been cleared to make way for Tramway Avenue two years later.

The Angel inn, Church Street, West Ham, date unknown. All Saints Church is in the background. Note the cyclist, pedalling majestically down the centre of the tram tracks. The Angel inn was rebuilt in 1910, and this view probably dates from about ten years before.

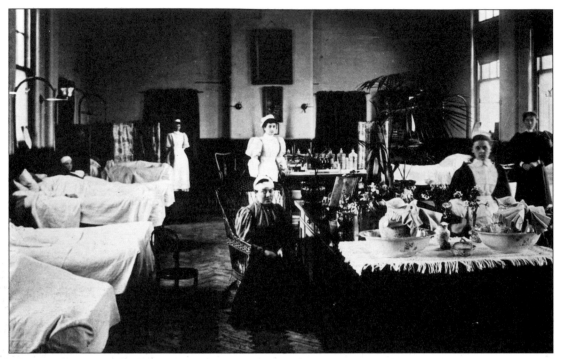

Two wards at West Ham Hospital, July 1900. The top view shows a ladies' ward; the bottom view shows a children's ward. Originally built as a smallpox hospital in Western Road, Plaistow, it was shortly to be replaced by a new Plaistow fever hospital, which was formed from the merger of two other hospitals in 1902.

A busy scene at the wharf, just south of Bow Bridge, April 1898. This was once the lowest of the crossing points over the River Lea and there had been a bridge here from the twelfth century. This bridge dated from 1835–9, with an echo of the original bow in its design, but it was soon to give way to a replacement, which was constructed between 1901 and 1906.

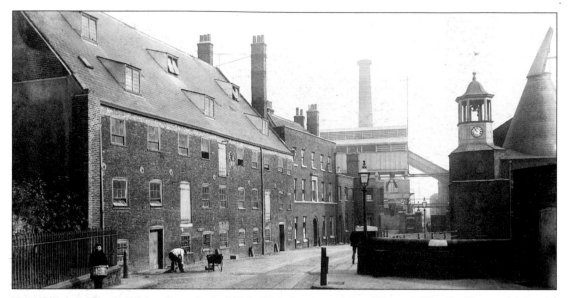

The Three Mills distillery, Stratford, 1900. This is part of the Three Mills distillery, which was situated on the island between the River Lea and Bow Creek. The works tramway runs past House Mill (left), and dated from 1776. Part of Clock Mill, which dated from 1817, is also visible. Once the property of Stratford Abbey, in the later sixteenth century there had been two watermills here, which were used for grinding corn and making gunpowder. The third, a windmill built in 1734, gave the site its name. From 1727 the mill site became a distillery, to be taken over by the Clerkenwell firm of J. and W. Nicholson in 1872. Fires in 1908 and 1920, together with bombing during the Second World War, destroyed many of the buildings, and distilling ceased in 1941. House Mill and Clock Mill are in the course of restoration as a museum.

Abbey Mill, Stratford, October 1900. The last of the mills was the Abbey flour mill, which was built on an island in the Channelsea River. First rebuilt in 1768, the large building was built in 1863–4 after a destructive fire. It lasted until the Second World War, when the area was bombed. Final clearance took place in the 1960s, when most of the site was taken to widen Abbey Road.

This timber-framed house formed part of Pinnock's Place, opposite St Mary's Church. There was an unproven tradition that it had once been the home of Admiral Benbow, and by the time of this photograph in 1895 it was the oldest house in the area. It was demolished within the next decade.

Rather grand for a kitchen fireplace? Essex Lodge, Greengate Street, Plaistow, was built using parts from the earlier Essex House, including a cut-down eighteenth-century door surround. The falcon crest is the badge of the Willyams family, who were the owners of Essex House in the 1760s.

The Hall, Balaam Street, Plaistow, September 1895. When Wire took this photograph this building was a private hospital. As Plaistow Hall it was owned in the early nineteenth century by Luke Howard, Quaker philanthropist, chemical manufacturer and meteorologist. Successive occupiers extended it, until it ceased to be a private house in the late 1890s. In use as a Church Army hostel and labour yard after the First World War, it was demolished for housing after 1945. The adjoining public house, the Greyhound, still stands.

Cumberland House and barn, Plaistow, August 1895. This house dated from the early seventeenth century, but the neighbouring barn was at least a century older and had once been a tithe barn for Stratford Langthorne Abbey. Measuring between 120 and 130 feet long, it was once the largest in Essex, but it was gradually allowed to fall into ruin and the remains were demolished in about 1905. Cumberland House lasted until 1936. The site is now covered by Gardner and Elkington roads.

Richmond House, Richmond Street, Plaistow, August 1895. This house was built in the early eighteenth century. By the time of this photograph, it was in an industrial neighbourhood and the adjoining building was Jeyes Sanitary Compound's factory. Jeyes had been formed in 1885 to make disinfectant that had been patented by the founder, John Jeyes, in 1879.

The splendid iron gates of Richmond House, Richmond Street, Plaistow, August 1895. Wire did not record the identity of the guardian standing alongside these gates – an aspirant for a part in a Sherlock Holmes mystery, perhaps? Richmond House lasted until 1930.

Stratford Broadway, Stratford, 1906. Wire took this photograph while standing by the entrance to the tramway depot, looking towards the Town Hall. The Swan Hotel was first recorded in 1631, but it was rebuilt in the eighteenth century and given a new front in the nineteenth century. It was entirely rebuilt in 1925.

Celebrations for Queen Victoria's Golden Jubilee, the Broadway, West Ham, June 1897. Locals are gathering round the 42 foot high monument to West Ham's Quaker benefactor, Samuel Gurney, which was erected in 1861. Besides the flags there were 'tasteful' shields and what the *Stratford Express* called 'striking devices' made up from coloured lamps and gas jets.

Shops on the Broadway, Stratford, July 1899. Wire took this photograph from the top of a horse tram, looking back towards a similar vehicle that had just picked its way through the delivery carts and hay wagons. West Ham's tram service had been started by the North Metropolitan, whose line from Aldgate to Stratford opened in 1870. West Ham Corporation had just begun the negotiations that were to lead to the takeover of the company's lines in West Ham and the electrification of the system from 1903.

The flags are out again, this time celebrating Mafeking Day on the Broadway, Stratford, 21 May 1900. The news has broken that Mafeking has been relieved from siege by the Boers during the Boer War. Two days later the *West Ham Guardian* reported enthusiasm bordering on madness, and when Councillor Spittle confirmed the news from the Town Hall after ten o'clock in the evening, the storm of cheering from the crowd could be heard a mile away. There was singing, dancing, impromptu bands and a bonfire on the street, before the crowds finally made their way home at dawn on Saturday morning.

The Broadway, Stratford, July 1900. Fodder arrives in the early morning, a reminder of the dependence people had on the horse at this time.

The Broadway, Stratford, June 1902. For the early worker, there was nothing like a cup of coffee from the coffee stall in front of 26 Stratford Broadway. Dunn's display drives home its sales message with the full force of assorted Victorian typography.

The Broadway, Stratford, Easter 1901. The shops at the corner of the High Road, opposite the Town Hall, were all closed for the Easter holiday when this photograph was taken. From left to right were John Baker Hawes fancy repository at Nos 372–4, Mr Greenhalgh the hosier, Nathans tobacconist, Wayland brothers watchmakers at No. 378, James Woods leather goods shop and William Edwards grocery. Great Eastern Road now sweeps north from this corner.

The Grove, Stratford, June 1902. In this early morning view, the lights and flags are out to celebrate the end of the Boer War on the Monday after peace was announced. As the day progressed, the shops in the Grove and along the High Street gradually increased their decorations – a plethora of electric lights, flags and Chinese lanterns.

The top of Romford Road, Stratford, April 1898, from level with the railings of St John's Church looking east along Romford Road. The tram tracks converge outside one of Young and Martin's showrooms. This firm of builder's merchants was founded in 1872 and grew rapidly during the next twenty years.

Rokeby House stood opposite St John's Church on the Broadway, Stratford, and was photographed by Wire in April 1898, in the last few months of its existence. Named after the Revd H.R. Rokeby, who owned it in 1853, the house dated from the early seventeenth century. In the nineteenth century, it served as a school, offices for the parish vestry and latterly as West Ham's first public library.

Stratford's Technical Institute had not long been open when it suffered considerable damage in a fire in 1899. The aftermath is seen in this view of October 1899. The institute had its origins in the technical classes of the Great Eastern Railway's Mechanics Institute, founded in 1851. West Ham's new institute included departments of science, engineering and art, as well as a special section for women. Repairs were soon made and the building was reopened in 1900.

Leyton lost little time in modernizing its tram service, electrifying the lines in 1906–7. A good crowd have come to see off the last horse tram in 1906, possibly on Leyton High Road.

A donkey barrow, near the Green Man inn, Leytonstone, 1901. Wire captured this barrow boy on camera during the Easter holiday.

LEYTON

Leyton was Wire's home borough. This view shows the Baker's Arms junction, looking north-east. The horse tram service along Lea Bridge Road had been established by the Lea Bridge, Leyton and Walthamstow Tramways Company in 1883. This photograph was taken in the year the service was taken over by Leyton Urban District Council.

The Great House, Leyton, July 1895. Leyton once had a large number of country houses, and one of the most splendid was the Great House, which stood opposite the sports ground on Leyton High Road. It was built a little before 1712 for Fisher Tench in dark red brick with dressings of lighter brickwork and stone. This view shows the garden front. Under later owners, the Olivers, the house was remodelled by the Adam brothers and the sash windows would have been added at the same time. After 1839 it was mostly let, and it was used at different times as a boarding house and an asylum. It was demolished in 1905 and flats now occupy the site.

Foundation stone laying, Davies Lane School, Leytonstone, May 1900. Dignitaries are gathering for the ceremony. The completed school opened for junior mixed and infants in the following year, the last of sixteen new schools opened by Leyton School Board between 1874 and 1903.

The entrance to Blue Row, Leyton High Road, October 1897. Grange Park Road is running off to the left. Blue Row originally referred to the buildings opposite the old vicarage, of which the fruit shop belonging to Henry Benton was one. Benton is about to take a delivery from the horse and cart, attracting a small audience. The horse tram has passed by safely on its way south, while the delivery boy and friend get on with their round.

Benton's shop, the High Street, Leyton, May 1905. Wire set up his camera at 4 o'clock one afternoon to take this photograph looking south from Blue Row. Henry Benton has put his shop frontage to best advantage to support his political ambitions in a council by-election in June. Benton won and served on Leyton UDC for several years but by the end of 1905 his shop had gone to allow for road improvements.

Two views of Blue Row, Leyton, May 1905. Wire completed his visual record of Blue Row's east side looking north (top) and south on the same day. The florist is doing a fine trade and even Dagley's Temperance and Refreshment Bar is attracting some attention. In the lower view a London County Council tram trundles towards the terminus just north of Leyton station. Trade is slow in the late afternoon and the woman and her dog keep a close eye on the escaping child.

Old buildings, opposite the Green, Leytonstone, April 1906. The Old Chestnut Tree Coffee House has just closed and has been temporarily taken over by T.J. Wardill & Son, builders.

The Red Lion inn, the High Road, Leytonstone, August 1889, looking north. This public house was originally the Robin Hood and was first recorded in 1670, the name changing by 1766. Wire took this photograph of the group of weatherboarded (and probably timber-framed) buildings the year before they were cleared. The replacement Red Lion inn and shops were designed by W.D. Church and completed in 1891.

Down the distant track on Horsey Island,
Kirby-le-Soken, July 1897.

INDEX

Note: where only one or two photographs of a place appear, only the name of the village is usually given. The index does not
include subject or place references made in the introduction and biographical notes on Alfred Wire.